The First 100 Years

An Illustrated History of the West Allis Fire Department

By Steven Hook, Fire Chief

The First 100 Years
An Illustrated History of the West Allis Fire Department

© 2006 by The West Allis Fire Department

All rights reserved. No part of this book may be reproduced or transmitted in any form or by any means, electronic or mechanical, including photocopying, recording, or by any information storage-and-retrieval system, without written permission from the publisher.

All notations of errors or omissions, author inquiries, permissions and rights concerning the contents of this book should be addressed to the West Allis Fire Department.

ISBN 0-9778061-0-3 (hardcover)
ISBN 978159598-903-1 (softcover; reprinted in 2022)

Publisher:	West Allis Fire Department
	7332 West National Avenue
	West Allis, WI 53214
	www.ci.west-allis.wi.us
	(414) 302-8900
	(414) 302-8927 (fax)

Content Reviewer:	Captain Bernard Burke, WAFD retired

Copies of this book may be obtained by contacting the West Allis Fire Department

> *The facts contained in this book were compiled from a variety of sources, including firefighter interviews; City of West Allis, West Allis Fire Department and West Allis Historical Society records; and media reports from the West Allis Star, The Milwaukee Journal and others. The information contained in this publication is presumed accurate, and is intended for reader entertainment, not necessarily historical reference. The author of this book and the West Allis Fire Department bear no responsibility for errors or omissions.*

Dedication

This book is dedicated to the entire "family" of the West Allis Fire Department.

This "family" includes all past and present members, their relatives and their friends; the many people who have contributed to shaping the history of the City of West Allis and the fire department including members of the Police and Fire Commission, Mayors and Alderpersons, and all of the people who have supported our efforts over <u>The First 100 Years</u>.

Acknowledgements

Special thanks to Captain Bernie Burke, WAFD retired, for his support, guidance and attention to detail. Bernie's commitment to collecting, restoring, and labeling historical photographs made this book possible. Without the West Allis Fire Department's unofficial "historian", the story of our department could not be told.

❖❖❖

The author wishes to acknowledge the help of the West Allis Historical Society, especially the late John Clow and Devan Gracyalny. The society tolerated several visits, and allowed scanning, copying and photographing of many documents in their collection. Also, the help of Deputy Chief Robert Schoenborn, and Captain Tony Sparacino, both WAFD retired, was invaluable in collecting and categorizing documents for this book.

❖❖❖

A recent history of the West Allis Fire Department would not be complete without acknowledging the support and behind-the-scenes persistency of a true friend of the department, Paul M. Murphy. As Common Council President and later as Municipal Judge, Paul ensured that the fire department was never neglected by city government, and that the citizens of our City and members of the department were armed with the necessary tools to provide the best service our people could afford. Thank you, Paul.

❖❖❖

Many of the department's accomplishments over the last ten years would not have happened without the encouragement and determination of the Police and Fire Commission, especially president Wayne Clark. Wayne insisted on meticulous attention to detail and challenged department leaders to constantly "raise the bar". The department's national accreditation and station remodeling projects were a credit to his persistence.

❖❖❖

Many of the photographs and newspaper articles used in this book came from the collection of Captain Jim Ley of the Milwaukee Fire Department. Thanks Jim, for your contributions.

❖❖❖

Many members of the department contributed to this book by photographing fire scenes and helping organize photos and information. The help of Lieutenant Dan Machowski, Captain Mike Bailey, Assistant Chiefs Gary Streicher and Marty King, Captain Ed Liska (retired), and FF Scott Liska was much appreciated.

❖❖❖

Finally, thanks to my family, especially my wife Mary, for her endless encouragement, and for enduring the years I spent gathering photos and staring into my computer produce this work.

Table of Contents

Chapter 1, Introduction: The History of West Allis   1

Chapter 2, The Fire Department   5

     Storing Fire Equipment Without a Firehouse   6
     The West Allis Volunteer Fire Department is Born   6
     Seat of Government   7
     Calling the Volunteers   8
     Horses and Harnesses   8
     False Alarms and Rapid Responses   9
     Responsibilities of the Fire Chief   9
     Reorganization   10
     Funding Assistance for the Early Fire Department   10
     Motorized Equipment   11
     City Growth Leads to Firefighter Pay Changes   12
     Fire Prevention Efforts   13
     Mutual Aid?   14
     A New Alarm System   14
     The Call Man System   15
     Full Paid Fire Department   17
     The Fire Department Needs a New Quarters   17
     Chief Burbach Dies   20
     Edwin Bryant Appointed Fire Chief   22
     First Master Mechanic Dies   27
     Fire Station/Police Station/Alarm Building Plans Change   27
     Emergency Medical Services   27
     Civil Defense   27
     Annexation and Growth   30
     Dispatching Fire Companies   35
     Bureau of Maintenance and Repair   37
     West Allis Industrial Fire Brigade   39
     Fire Prevention, Inspection and Code Enforcement   41
     Paramedics   52
     Survive Alive   56
     Hazardous Materials Level B   62
     Technical Rescue Team   65
     Tunnel Rescue   68
     International Accreditation   68

Semiautomatic Cardiac Defibrillation	69
Public Access Defibrillation	72
Thermal Imaging	72
CPAT (Candidate Physical Ability Testing)	73
Chapter 3, The Fire Stations	**75**
On the Move...A Timeline of West Allis Fire Stations	76
Fire Station No. 1, 7332 W. National Avenue	79
Fire Station Remodeling	85
The "Blue Ooze"	87
Remodeling Plans Back on Track	87
Fire Station No. 1, 7300 W. National Avenue	89
Fire Administration Building, 7332 W. National Avenue	99
Fire Station No. 2, 2040 S. 67th Place	103
Station 2's Next 50 Years	106
Fire Station No. 2 remodeling	106
Fire Station No. 3, 10830 W. Lapham Avenue	114
Fire Station No. 3 remodeling	114
Alternative Fire Station	114
Project Delays Cause Weather Problems	120
Finally Back in Quarters	120
Chapter 4, Fire Apparatus	**121**
Ambulances	155
Support Vehicles	159
History of Fire Apparatus	162
Chapter 5, The Fire Chiefs	**165**
Chapter 6, Personnel	**169**
2006 Administrative Staff	169
2006 West Allis Fire Department	170
Members of the WA Fire Department, Past & Present	177
Members of the WA Board of Police and Fire Commissioners	185
Chapter 7, Scrapbook	**187**

Forward

The City of West Allis developed as a result of the rapid industrialization of southeastern Wisconsin. The growth of our community required a fire department capable of protecting the lives and property of the City's many new residents and one that could protect the many factories and workplaces that employed most of them.

The West Allis Fire Department began as an industrial fire brigade at the new Allis Chalmers plant. The brigade was supplemented by volunteers from the community who were called into service by a series of blasts from the plant's whistle.

The industrial brigade has grown into a modern, technologically-equipped workforce capable of mitigating any emergency from a simple room and contents fire to serious medical emergencies, hazardous materials incidents, and even deep tunnel rescue alarms.

"The First 100 Years" is a celebration of the dynamic development of the fire department as an element of a City system that is in the midst of a dramatic redevelopment. Many of the City's industrial giants have moved or closed, and service agencies have taken their places.

Population demographics continue to change as well. The City has more senior living units than ever, and many homes and buildings are aging. Transportation routes are busier than ever, and new businesses have replaced or remodeled many of the factories built over a century ago. These developments have tested the fire department's ability to enlist new technology and to continuously adapt its operational tactics.

We are proud to acknowledge that the fire department is a reflection of our community. The same work ethic that has driven residents to produce superior industrial products and attract high quality service providers has motivated firefighters to continuously "raise the bar" with the services we provide and the quality with which we provide them.

West Allis firefighters have been innovators, and have been quick to jump at the opportunity to provide new services. We placed the first paramedic unit in southeastern Wisconsin into service in 1973. We developed Wisconsin's first "Survive Alive" program, and we were the first department in Wisconsin to equip basic life providers with defibrillators. We had the first public-access defibrillator program in our area, and in 2003, we became the first career department in Wisconsin to earn international accreditation. We are one of the very few departments nationwide, that equip all fire attack companies with thermal imaging cameras to speed rescue and fire attack.

Nearly five hundred men and women have worked to help the fire department continuously improve the level of service we provide to residents and visitors of West Allis. Our community is safer as a result of the efforts of these individuals. Their work has been effective because of the support of numerous members of the Police and Fire Commission, alderpersons, mayors and a supportive community.

This book was written to document the history of the West Allis Fire Department's first one-hundred years. It highlights the many accomplishments of our members in the context of the support of our community.

Chapter 1

Introduction: The City of West Allis

The history of the West Allis begins as far back as the early 1800's. In 1835, Ebenezer Cornwall, Ruben Strong and Peter Marlett traveled west from New York State, through Ohio and into Chicago. While they were in Chicago, they heard people talking about a district to the north, called "Milwaukie". Intrigued, they decided to visit the area and were especially impressed with a densely wooded region to the west. It was scattered with fresh water springs and the rapidly flowing Honey Creek.

Honey Creek Settlement

Cornwall, Strong and Marlett were so impressed that they founded the "Honey Creek Settlement". They brought their families from New York to join them and began clearing land to raise produce for sale in Milwaukee markets.

Other settlers began to arrive soon afterward. Well-traveled Indian trails became common thoroughfares for the early settlers. The Mukwanago Plank Road ran directly through the area and crossed several other trails near the present S. 61st Street and W. National Avenue. The intersection of these trails became known as the "Old Five Points" and. The Five Points grew a busy trade and shopping attraction.

Developers and businessmen were also attracted to the Honey Creek settlement. Anthony Duovalle and Spencer Case began a local lumber business and built a sawmill. Within a few years, Honey Creek boasted several homes, a blacksmith shop, post office and a log chapel shared by local Baptists and Episcopalians. A log school was built and mail was delivered by stagecoach

In 1860, a brick school was built at the present site of S. 84th Street and W. National Avenue. Seven children attended the first classes, but the new community had become popular and was growing fast (Today, the schoolhouse is the home of the West Allis

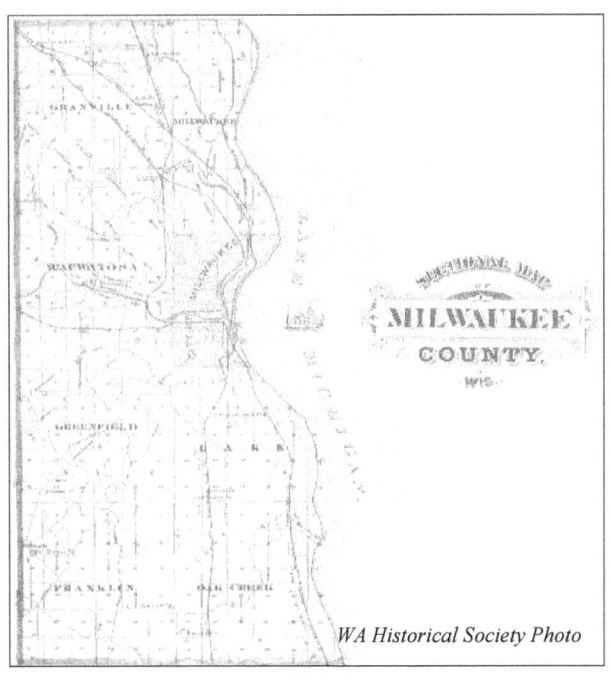

WA Historical Society Photo

1876
Milwaukee County Sectional Map

Historical Society, and is at the center of the City of West Allis).

By 1880 the Chicago-Northwestern Railroad's Madison Division track stretched through the Honey Creek settlement. The "North Greenfield" station stood near today's intersection of S. 82nd St and W. National Avenue, in Greenfield township. When the area was surveyed and platted in 1887 the

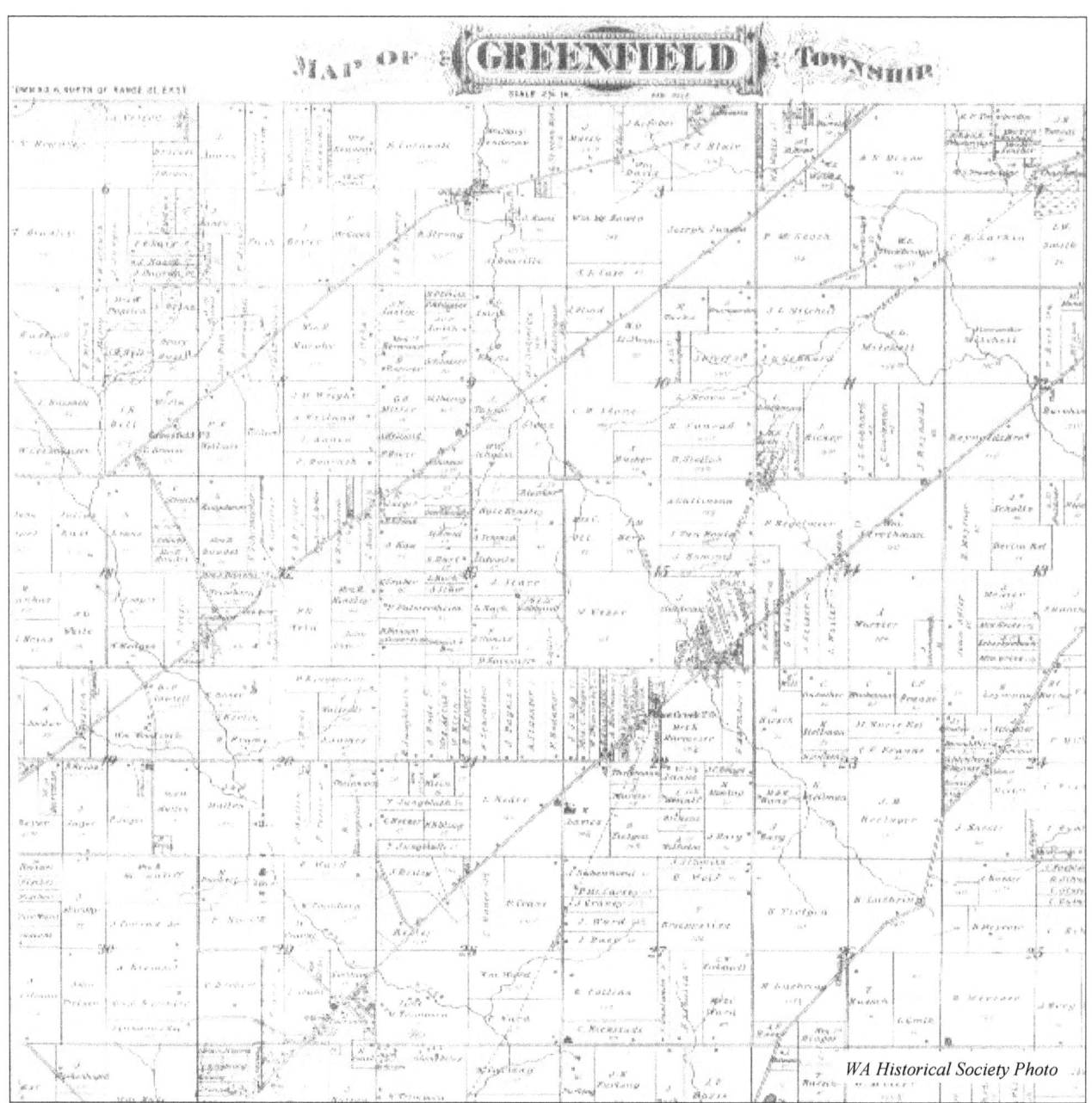

*1876
Greenfield Township Map*

Honey Creek settlement became better known as North Greenfield.

State Fair

Wisconsin's rich agricultural heritage was displayed annually at the Agricultural Society's State Fair. From 1853 to 1890, the Fair was held at various sites including Janesville, Madison and Milwaukee. In 1891, the Agricultural Society purchased the Stevens dairy farm, complete with the family mansion, several smaller homes and outbuildings. The land was bounded on the north by the railroad. On this land, the Wisconsin State Fair found a permanent home in North Greenfield.

Although the estate burned in 1893, the State Fair remained. New buildings were erected, and the fair continued its annual event into the present day.

Allis Chalmers Company c1910

Transportation Improves and Industrialization Comes to North Greenfield

In order to make access to the area easier, the Milwaukee Street Car Company extended its lines west to the Fair grounds. This introduction of improved transportation facilities as well as easy railroad access accelerated the growth of North Greenfield.

At the turn of the twentieth century, southeastern Wisconsin was in the center of the nation's industrial revolution. Developers in this heavily industrial area were looking for places to establish themselves and enhance their opportunities.

On November 25, 1900, Stutley I. Henderson contacted Charles Allis of the Edward P. Allis Company, and offered property for the expansion of his business. Allis' plant on Milwaukee's Clinton Street was badly in need of space. Hendersen could provide access to both the Milwaukee and the Northwestern Railroads and he thought this site would be perfect for Allis to expand his business.

The Edward P. Allis Company bought one hundred acres of Henderson's land for $25,000. Soon afterward, the company began construction of a huge plant, which that become the Allis Chalmers Corporation. The plant opened on November 26, 1900, employing 3,000 workers and producing $6,000,000 of machinery annually.

Other successful manufacturing plants joined Allis Chalmers in North Greenfield. Among these were the Rosenthal Corn Husker Company, the Fred Prescott Company, the Kearney and Trecker Corporation and the Kempsmith Company.

The Village of West Allis is Incorporated

By 1902, the area had a population of 1,018 and civic leaders felt the need to provide community services by incorporating as a village. A village boundary was selected that began at the growing shopping area near today's S. 56th Street and W. Greenfield Avenue, and stretched westward to include portions of the towns of Greenfield and Wauwatosa.

The village of "West Allis" was legally incorporated on May 31, 1902, and an election of officers was held on July 23rd. Frederick W. Henderson became the Village's first President.

Frederick Hendersen

Governor Declares West Allis a City

West Allis' rapid growth was continuing and by 1906 the village's population had dou-

1903 Village Council
Some notable members of the Village's second council were the Fire Chief/Village Marshall Eugene Braunschweiger (seated at far left), 2nd Village President Theodore Trecker (seated, center), 1st Village President Frederick Henderson (seated, far right), and future Mayor Frank Baldwin (standing, third from right)

bled. On April 12, 1906, Wisconsin Governor J. O. Davidson declared West Allis a City of the fourth class with a population of 2,306 and land area of 2,400 acres.

West Allis' first Mayor, Frank E. Walsh soon began laying the groundwork for the city's civic development. On April 17, 1906 the Common Council directed Mayor Walsh to appoint his City officers. Among these were a City Attorney, City Clerk, Board of School Commissioners, two policemen, a City Physician, Street Commissioner, Police Chief, and Fire Chief.

A new City had been established; a Fire Chief had been appointed; and the West Allis Fire Department was about to begin its first year.

One hundred years later, our story begins...

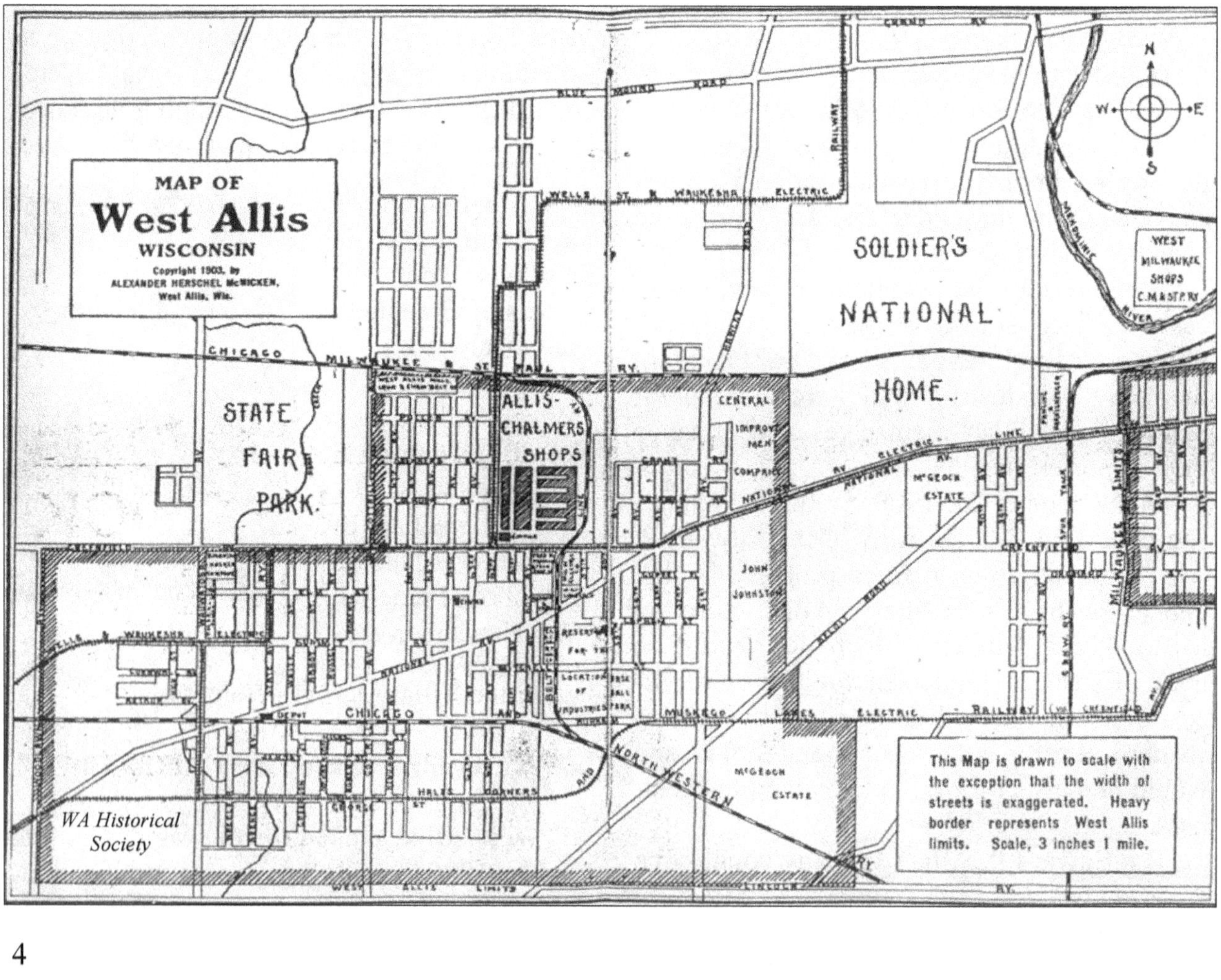

Chapter 2

The Fire Department

On September 23, 1903 the Village Board, lead by President Theodore Trecker (of the Kearney & Trecker Manufacturing Corporation) authorized the borrowing of $50,000 for fire protection and "to supply fresh residential water". The Board sought a contract to build a system of water works complete with all the necessary pumps, mains, buildings, reservoirs and appliances. In a special election on October 19th, 1903 citizens voted at the usual polling place on the southwest corner of Greenfield and 63rd Avenues, from 6:00 p.m. to 7:00 p.m. and approved bonding for the project.

Although the Village had procured a new water system, the fire department wasn't "organized" until the Village became a City of the fourth class on April 12, 1906. Before that, many local citizens volunteered with the Allis Chalmers Fire Brigade.

A December 14th 1904 resolution conveyed the Village's official thanks to the

Hand-drawn hose carts were suitable for carrying at least 450 feet of jacketed hose, a solid stream brass nozzle and chemical extinguisher. A gong mounted inside the wheel gave warning to pedestrians that firefighters were responding

Allis Chalmers Fire Department for "...the efficient services rendered by them..." at a fire occurring on December 8th.

West Allis was growing rapidly, and the Village Board began preparing to handle their own fire emergencies. While the Allis Chalmers Brigade was helpful, the Village knew that an organized fire department would soon be necessary. In November of 1905, they authorized ads in the "Milwaukee Daily News" and the "West Allis Republican" to accept sealed bids for:

- 2,000 feet of 2 ½ inch jacketed fire hose, complete with couplings,
- 6 fire nozzles suitable for coupling upon the 2 ½ inch hose,
- 1 combination hose, chemical and ladder wagon arranged for a chemical tank of not less than 40 gallons, that could carry 2 six-gallon hand fire extinguishers and at least 800 feet of 2 ½" jacketed hose
- 2 hand-drawn hose carts suitable for carrying at least 450 feet of jacketed hose
- Six 6-gallon chemical fire extinguishers
- Six 12-foot and six 16-foot ladders for fire purposes (the ladders were ordered to be constructed such that each 12-foot section could be attached to each 16-foot section to form an extension ladder)

On December 13, 1905 the Board hired the American Light and Water Company to enhance the new water works system by placing hydrants on 48th, 62nd, and State Avenues where they intersected National Avenue. And two weeks later, on December 28, 1905 the Board approved the purchase of:

- 1000 feet of Red Cross Brand of Eureka fire hose,
- 500 feet of Princeton Brand of Badger Machinery fire hose and
- 500 feet of Peninsular Brand of Empire Rubber Manufacturing fire hose

All of the hose cost 80¢ per foot. The Board required the use of aluminum couplings fitted with Milwaukee special fire hose coupling thread.

With the new equipment, the groundwork for the Village's volunteer fire department had been laid.

Storing Fire Equipment Without a Firehouse

New firefighting equipment was arriving quickly, but the Village had yet to build a firehouse. So on March 27, 1906, the Board ordered that:

1. the combined hose and chemical wagon would be kept at the livery barn of G. H. Jung (the local undertaker) on State Ave. for $2 per month,
2. one two-wheeled hose cart and equipment was to be kept at the barn of Frank Rock on 65th Ave. near Greenfield Ave. for $2 per month, and
3. one two-wheeled hose cart was to be kept at the barn of M. Peters at the corner of 53rd Ave. and Greenfield Ave. (Mr. Peters agreed to store the fire equipment at no charge)

The West Allis Volunteer Fire Department is Born

When West Allis became a City on April 12, 1906, Mayor Frank Walsh and the Common Council began appointing various City officers. Eugene Braunschweiger was appointed Chief of the Volunteer Fire Department on May 9, 1906. Braunschweiger had been serving as Village Marshall, with one deputy, William Strong. Mayor Walsh appointed George Leonard Chief of Police.

The first meeting of the West Allis Volunteer Fire Department was held on May 15, 1906. At this meeting, the following appointments were approved:

Eugene Braunschweiger	Chief Engineer
Robert Miller	Assistant Chief
H. S. Berninger	Assistant Chief
Arthur Johnson	Captain, Co. No. 1
Charles Eiche	Captain, Co. No. 2
E. J. Neeb	Captain, Co. No. 3
Peter H. Burbach	Lieutenant, Co. No. 1
Charles Donnelly	Lieutenant, Co. No. 2
Walter Ottoway	Lieutenant, Co. No. 3
John Gohres	Lieutenant, Co. No. 3
S. C. McCorkle, M.D.	Department Surgeon

Seat of Government

To provide a home for the new City government, the Central Improvement Company donated land on the northwest corner of 64th and National Avenues (currently S. 73rd St. & W. National Avenue) and a two story masonry building was completed in September of 1906. The building served as City Hall, fire and police station, jail, School Board meeting hall and home for any other City function.

City Ordinance 39, passed on May 9, 1906, fixed the salaries of City officials:

City Clerk:	$83.83 per month
City Attorney	$75.00 per month
Physician	$12.30 per month
Street Commissioner	$65.00 per month

c1908: West Allis Volunteer firefighters gather with West Allis police officers. Asst. Chief Edwin Bryant is seated in the second row, third from the left and Chief Burbach is seated in the second row, fourth from the right. Al Lecher is in the middle of row three. Seated in the front row is (l to r) William J. Wassweiler, Marshall Eugene Braunschweiger and Eugene Phalen, tavern owner and future (1930's) part owner of the Allis Theater.

Fire Chief	$50.00 per year
Each fireman	$20.00 per year
Police Chief	$65.00 per month
(must have phone at his expense)	
Each policeman	$55.00 per month
City Treasurer	$60.00 per month
Mayor	$75.00 per month
Each Alderman	$15.00 per month

To help the Volunteer Fire Department the Common Council quickly authorized other necessary items like a sufficient supply of soda for the chemical wagons, a hand chemical extinguisher and a gong for the Chief's buggy. They also gave the firefighters authority to tap water mains to fight fires.

Calling the Volunteers

To alert the volunteers, the Council ordered the City to adopt a fire alarm system and to purchase a good fire alarm whistle as selected by the Council's Fire Department Committee. The whistle was to be a 2-inch pipe whistle of 120 psi., attached to the boiler of the Allis-Chalmers Company. In addition, a code of alarms was to be developed "at the earliest possible moment", to designate the location of fires. The Fire Department Committee was ordered to arrange the signals with the manager of the Allis-Chalmers Company so they wouldn't conflict with any system of signals or alarms in use by the company.

Horses and Harnesses

At first, the firefighters relied upon local residents and businesses to volunteer horses, but they weren't always available. Therefore, shortly after officially organizing the department, the Common Council authorized the Board of Public Works to advertise for bids

for a team of horses. Sealed bids, not to exceed $500 for each horse specified that the horses must weigh between 1400 and 1600 pounds, and be 5 to 8 years old. The City also purchased drop harnesses for the team.

False Alarms and Rapid Responses

With a rapidly developing fire department, council members were becoming concerned about false alarms causing the unnecessary response of firefighters and their new horse and wagons. They voted to establish a penalty of up to $25 for "...anyone causing a false alarm or other bells, horns, bugles or triangles that tended to obstruct the streets".

Responsibilities of the Fire Chief

At the time of his appointment, Chief Braunschweiger the only paid employee of the fire department. All others were volunteers. The Common Council determined that the Chief's duties were to keep all apparatus and supplies in safe and proper condition. He was to care for and clean the brass work of the chemicals and hose carts, dry the hose and fill the chemicals. If he "...gave faithful attention to his duties", he would be paid $25 per month.

An old-timer's recollection of the events of the period is recorded in files of the West Allis Historical Society:

> "A volunteer fire department of some thirty men was organized in charge of Chief Eugene Braunschweiger, an energetic man, who feared nothing and was very proud of his officers. He had his old horse, Barney, and a buckboard, Gubby. He

made a drop harness. He had a large bell under the floorboards and an alarm clock, which he would set for 2:00 a.m. for practice and speed. His good wife was nearly nuts when the alarm clock went off and Brauny dashed out of bed, hitched up Barney and "Bong! Bong!" raced up National Avenue, waking up all the neighbors.

Joe Gargen's place on old 57th Avenue caught fire. The hose would not quite reach, but the department smashed windows to let the smoke out, then chopped the burning parts from the building. The next day Braunschweiger demanded more hose from Mayor Walsh, who kidded him. Brauny got peeved and asked, "Do you vant I should get fires out mit mine own hose?"

Well, Braunschweiger finally retired and Assistant Chief Peter Burbach was appointed. The department grew from hand-drawn to horse-drawn apparatus and better equipment and the boys had uniforms. When the fire whistle blew, every man responded. Herman Matz ran home to get his uniform and rubber clothes. In all fires something was saved. When the fires were out, all hands retired to Burbach's bar and when all was accounted for, the fire was officially declared out, and all blunders were discussed."

Fire destroyed the State Fair Park grandstand August 3, 1914

Reorganization

The volunteer fire department completed a set of bylaws in January of 1907, and in February, a reorganization of the membership occurred. Peter H. Burbach was elected Chief with two assistants, Robert Miller and Art Johnson. Chief Braunschweiger resigned to become the City's Fire Marshall. Peter H. Burbach was officially appointed Fire Chief on February 14, 1907.

Funding Assistance for the Early Fire Department

On April 27, 1907, the Common Council passed an ordinance requiring the City Clerk to "...transfer the money paid by insurance companies through their respective solicitors and agents, being the legal 2% levy on gross premiums for the support and maintenance of the fire department, to the Fire Department Treasurer."

On June 12th, 1913, The Common Council ordered that saloon licensing fees (up to $6,000) were to be appropriated for the police and fire departments, with the excess going into the City's general fund.

Ordinance 242, passed on August 25, 1913, formally established the "Police and Fire Department Fund", and required that all money raised for the support of the police and fire departments was to be placed in this fund, and the expenses of the departments were to be paid from the fund. .

Some of the City's first fire fighters gather for a photo in their protective equipment. Left to right are: John Fagg, George Burbach?, 2 unknowns, John Petrie?, Florian Luckow and Eugene Phalen?

Motorized Equipment

West Allis firefighters responded to alarms with horse-drawn chemical and ladder wagons, and with hand-drawn hose carts for the first ten years. On November 11, 1915 a Seagrave 750 gallon per minute pumper was purchased. This truck, the department's first motorized apparatus was put into service in 1916.

With the delivery of this new pumper, the Common Council authorized the Board of Police and Fire Commissioners to hire an "Auto Truck Driver". The driver was to be paid $85.00 per month

Chief Burbach quickly saw the advantages

A parade in West Allis without fire fighters would certainly be unusual, and the one in this photograph from around 1915 is no exception. A daring fire fighter climbs the "church raise", a staple of early training exercises.

of motorized equipment and urged the City to continue replacing the horse-drawn apparatus with motorized vehicles. In one early effort, the Chief recommended a cost-efficient method to equip the horse-drawn ladder truck with a motorized chassis. He tried to show that he could save money and provide a benefit for the City.

Although Chief Burbach's retrofit effort was unsuccessful, the department was able to buy a Seagrave service truck in 1921 to compliment the 1916 pumper.

City Growth Leads to Firefighter Pay Changes

Chief Burbach continued managing his department in a rapidly growing City. World

West Allis Fire Fighters have a history of participating in competitive events. Long before the modern day softball tournaments, our members were bringing home the championship trophy. This aged newspaper clipping proudly displays West Allis Volunteers at their best in a volunteer firefighter competition. The field across from the Allis Chalmers Company on S. 70th Street in West Allis was the tournament site for the events pictured here.

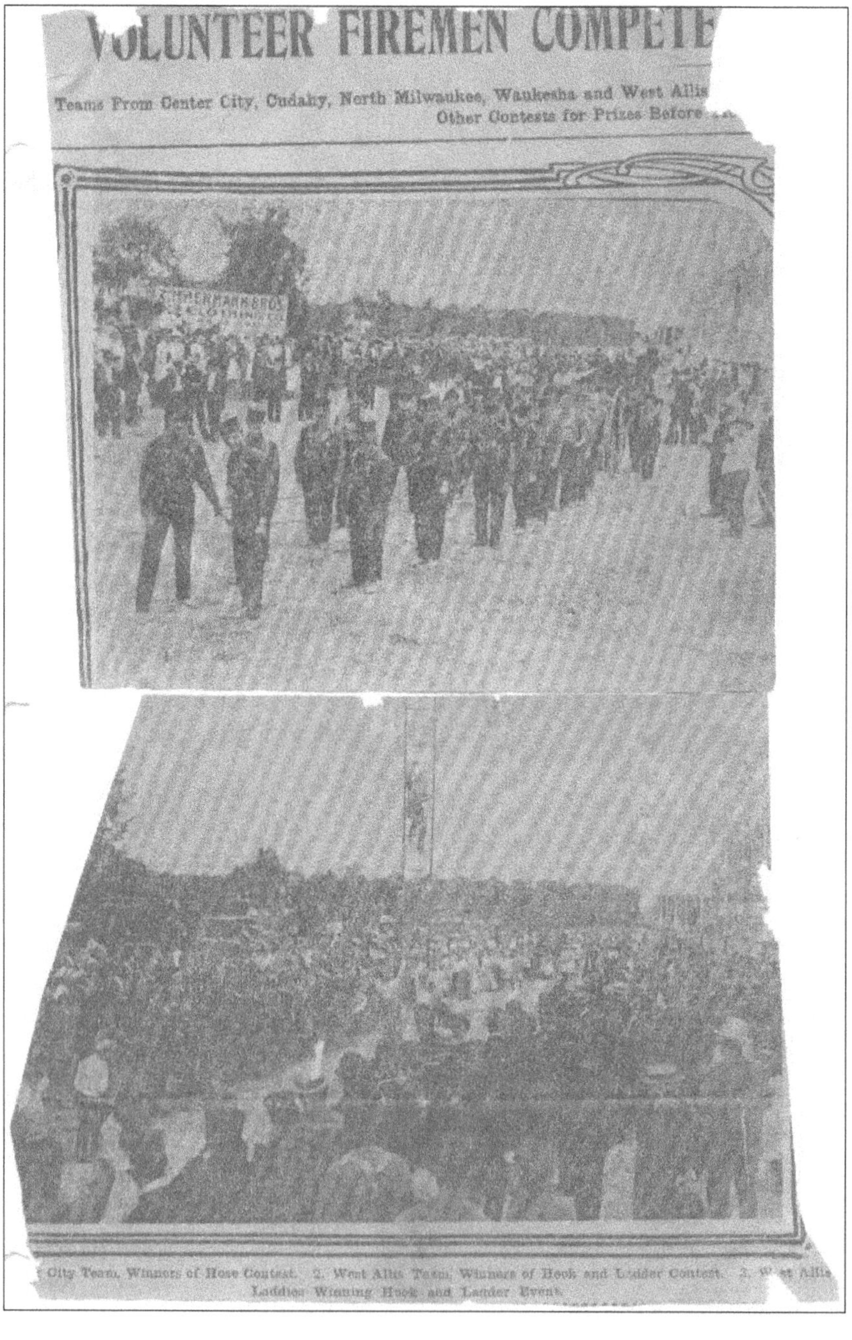

VOLUNTEER FIREMEN COMPETE

Teams From Center City, Cudahy, North Milwaukee, Waukesha and West Allis
Other Contests for Prizes Before ...

City Team, Winners of Hose Contest. 2. West Allis Team, Winners of Hook and Ladder Contest. 3. West Allis Laddies Winning Hook and Ladder Event.

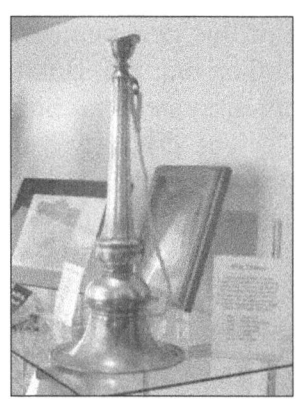

The traveling trophy from these early local events was a silver horn, currently on display at our headquarters.

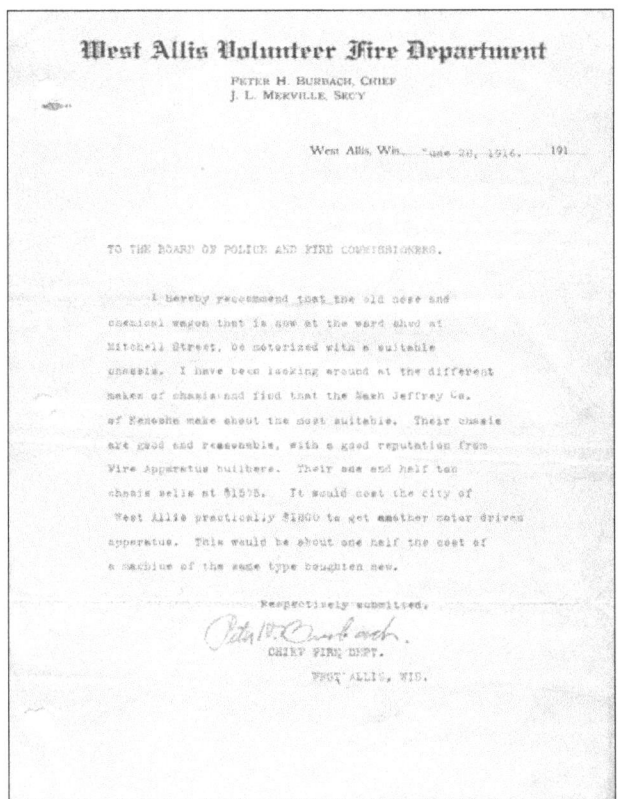

Chief Burbach, realizing the value of motorized equipment, quickly urged the City to consider fitting the horse-drawn ladder wagon with a used motorized chassis

War I was creating a demand for machinery and equipment that was produced in the factories of West Allis, and industry here was booming. With this industrial growth came a rapid increase in the population of West Allis and a corresponding increase in new homes.

The fire department was undergoing some changes as well. The entirely-volunteer fire department had become a memory and City leaders were now paying for parts of the department's staffing. The department was using "Call Men" to keep staffing at sufficient levels.

On August 1, 1919, firefighter salaries were adjusted. "Regular Firemen" were paid according to their years of service. They received $1200 in their first year, $1300 in their second, and $1500 in their third year with the department.

Fire Prevention Efforts

As time went by, City officials began to look at potential fire problems more seriously, resulting in several fire prevention laws. Ordinance No. 475, passed on September 23, 1919, prohibited lighting of fires within 25 feet of any building or structure. A person could be fined $1 to $5 for each of-

This postcard was originally postmarked January 8, 1912. It was sent to Chief Henry Nelson in 1957 by Fred Secosh, after Secosh had found it in a farm in Pewaukee

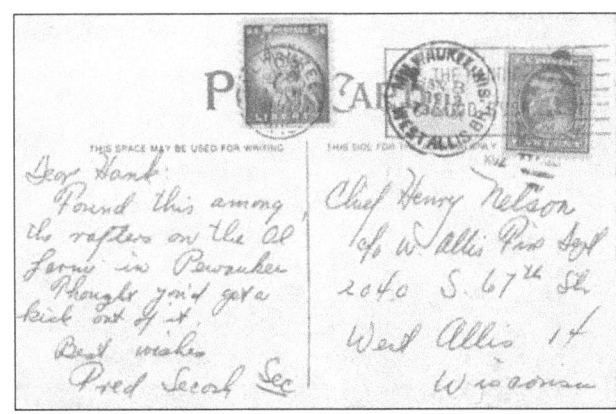

fense. In addition, the Mayor, Police Chief, Fire Chief or any alderman could restrain or prohibit fireworks or bonfires whenever a danger was perceived.

Chief Burbach and members of the West Allis Volunteer Fire Department pose with their newly delivered 1916 Seagrave 750 GPM Pumper. This was the first motorized fire apparatus for the young department.

On the heals of that action, another ordinance secured the right of way of certain vehicles. A person could be fined $10 to $25 for interfering with the progress of fire vehicles. All vehicles, including streetcars were ordered to yield. But the right of way ordinance did not apply to "...vehicles carrying U.S. mail."

The department's 1916 Seagrave pumper undergoes a serious pump test

Mutual Aid

Even before the 1920's, West Allis firefighters were responding to neighboring communities frequently enough for City leaders to bill for those responses. In order to receive West Allis services, a City, Town or Village was required to deposit $100 with the City Clerk in advance. For each service request, $25 was taken from the account. When the original $100 was depleted, another deposit was required. In 1922, the deposit and fee amounts doubled.

A New Alarm System

A Police and Fire Alarm System was approved on January 1, 1916 to make it easier for citizens to report fires or police emergencies using telegraph technology. The alarm system was intended to supplement the horn system in place at Allis Chalmers since 1906. The superintendent of the new system was

In March of 1917, the West Allis Volunteer Fire Department celebrated their tenth anniversary at the Allis Chalmers Clubhouse, a popular gathering place. The site is now a Milwaukee Area Technical College parking lot across from 1200 S. 70th St.

August C. Smith, and the inaugural alarm occurred at 8:55 P.M on May 10th. The system provided years of service for the department and was expanded over time to include call boxes around the city.

The Call Man System

One of the most significant steps en route to becoming a full time, full paid fire department was the start of the Call Man System. This system employed a few people on a full paid basis and was supplemented by part-time staff and "Call Men". Call Men were required to be available when called in time of emergency and were paid $15 per month.

Ordinance No. 612, passed on February 10, 1922 acknowledged that the growth and development of the City of West Allis had made it impractical to continue the Volunteer Fire Department. The ordinance disbanded the volunteer department and discontinued all of its duties and functions. The "foreman" of the department was directed to disband the organization, and all earlier resolutions or ordinances that had appropriated money for the department were repealed.

The last regular meeting of the West Allis

The final page of the West Allis Volunteer Fire Department ledger shows a final disbursement of funds. Note the final 11 cents, given to Edwin Bryant, caretaker of the department cat, for milk

Volunteer Fire Department was held on February 28, 1922. At that meeting, all assets of the department ($206.30) were distributed among the active members. Even the department's cat benefited as the last 11¢ were given to Edwin Bryant to buy milk.

On February 18, 1922, Ordinance No. 615 ordered the reorganization of the West Allis Fire Department. The new department was to consist of one Chief, who would "...respond to all fires and perform the duties of his office...", and six regular firemen, who were to "...devote their full time to the West Allis Fire Department". These paid members were in addition to the 12 "Call Men" who were appointed a week earlier when the volunteer fire department was disbanded.

As the department continued to grow, several other positions were added. In early 1923, one full paid Assistant Chief and one full paid Captain were added to the department. And in July of 1924, Ordinance 736 created the position of "Master Mechanic".

The Master Mechanic was considered essential because by 1924 the department owned "...automobiles and fire apparatus worth a considerable amount of money." According to the Council ordinance, "...It is considered 'expedient' that the position of Master Mechanic be created. The salary of the Master mechanic is the same as other firemen. The Police and Fire Commission shall

The volunteer fire department was abolished by ordinance, and replaced by a "Call Man" system on February 28, 1922

appoint the Master Mechanic and he is under their control." Charles Clunie was appointed Master Mechanic.

The Call Man System operated until 1925, and the members are listed below:

Original paid members:

Peter Burbach, Chief	Part-time
Edwin Bryant, Asst Chief	Full paid
Joseph Hayes, Captain	Full paid
Herman Matz, Lieutenant	Full paid
Charles Clunie, Pipeman	Full paid
George Burbach, Pipeman	Full paid
Barney Peterson, Pipeman	Full paid

Later entries to the paid service:

Joseph Charles	6/15/1922
John Petrie	3/16/1923
Joseph Gimmler	5/10/1923
Florian Luckow	2/1/1924

Call Men:

Henry Leitzke	Byron Stuart
Anthony Beres	John Krahn
Fred Glittenberg	John Merville
William Seeger	John Hoekenson
Fred Franson	Ralph Bates
Ben Franson	

Full Paid Fire Department

On January 8, 1925, the West Allis Common Council passed Ordinance No. 774, establishing a full-paid fire department. The new action repealed Ordinance 611 which had begun the "Call Man" system. It retroactively took effect on January 1st. At the same time, Ordinance No. 775 created the full time position of Fire Chief. The West Allis Fire Department had officially become fully paid.

The Fire Department Needs a New Quarters

Establishing a fully paid fire department demonstrated the City's commitment to providing a high level of fire protection, but the small quarters housing the new department was rapidly becoming inadequate. On July 1, 1926 the West Allis Star reported that the Police and Fire Commission had recommended that the Common Council purchase a parcel of land on the corner of 66th Avenue and National Avenue (today's S. 74th St. & W. National Ave.) for a new fire station. This property was right next door to the current fire station, and the land was vacant.

Under the plan, the cost for the land would

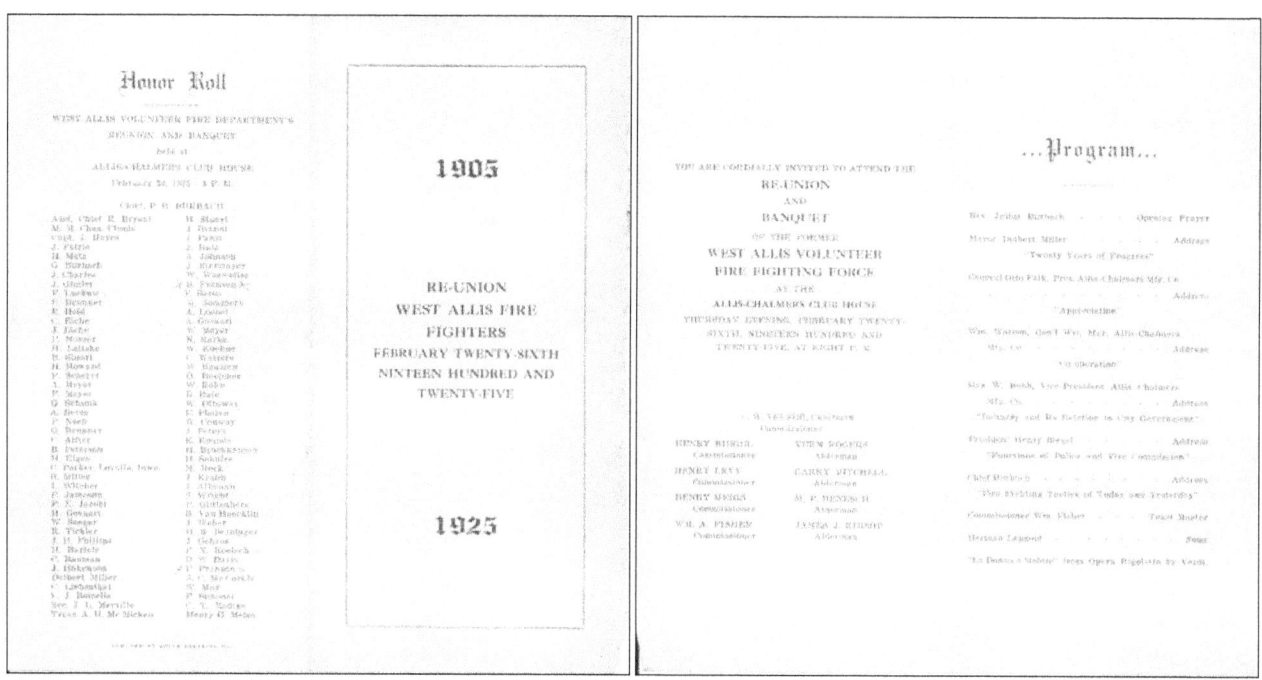

Souvenir Program from the West Allis Volunteer Fire Department's 20th Anniversary Reunion and Banquet, February 26, 1925

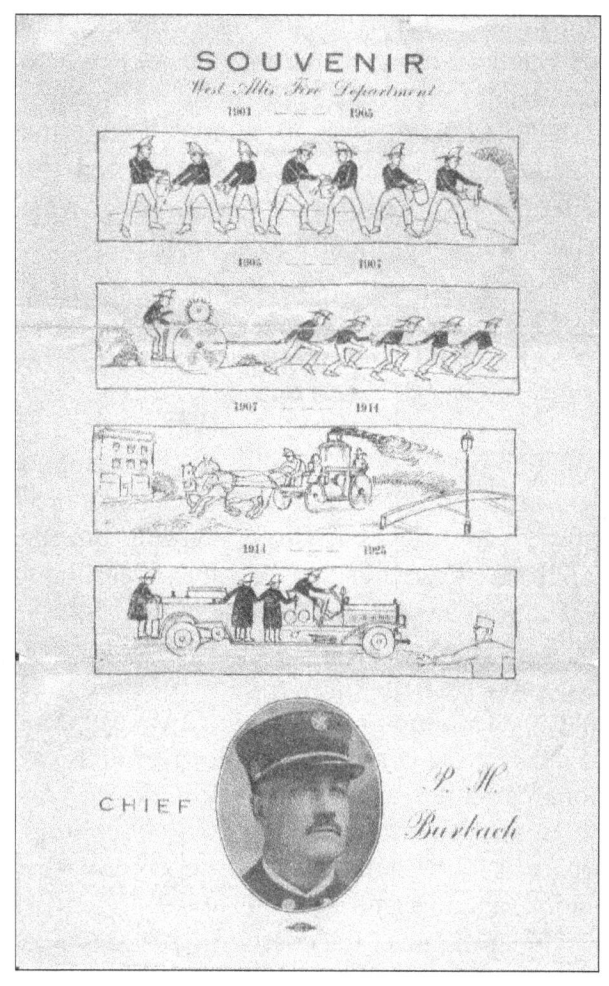
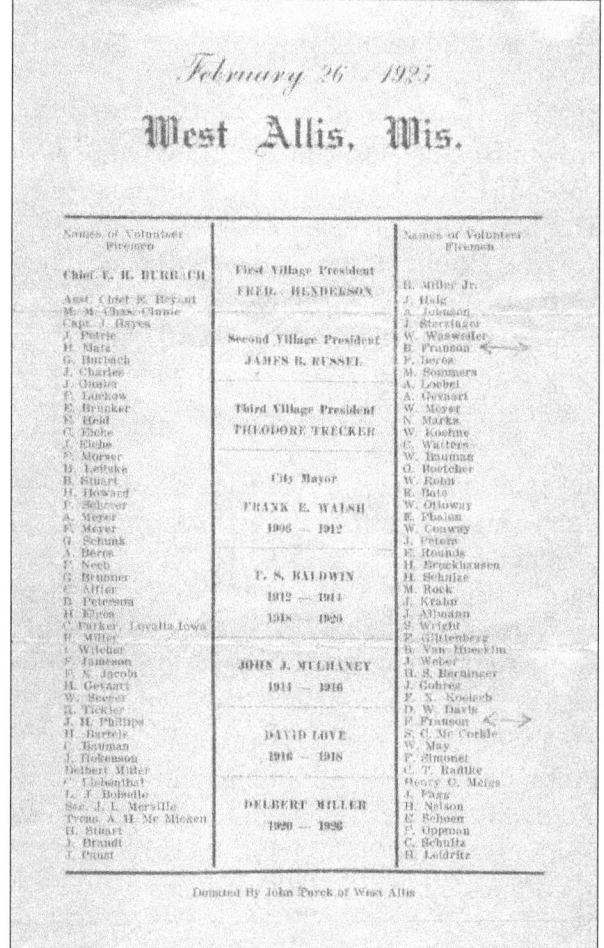

First Full-Paid Fire Department of West Allis, 1925
In front of their quarters at 609 S. 65th Street (present S. 73rd St. and W. National Ave., camera is looking west.)

L to R: Joe Gimler, Frank Oppmann, Bob Miller, Florian Luckow, Charles Clunie, John Petrie, CT Joseph Hayes, Herman Matz, Henry Nelson. Seated in 3rd vehicle: Joe Charles, John Fagg. Standing: AC Edwin Bryant, Harry Leideritz, George Burbach, Elmer Schoen, Charles Schultz, Chief Peter Burbach

not exceed $3500. The lot was a portion of a subdivision being developed by the Central Improvement Company.

Fire station plans were drawn up by Lindl and Schuette, a Milwaukee architectural firm. Joseph Lindl's design for Kenosha's Fire Station No. 4, had attracted the attention of Chief Burbach as being revolutionary in design. The new plans for West Allis' station were called "state of the art" and "progressive" for 1926. But getting the job done was a long and difficult task. The project was delayed by politically-motivated arguments, questionable contract appropriations, allegations of "bid-tampering", funding difficulties, state law challenges and even a "north-siders" versus "south-siders" dispute.

After four years of debate and staunch persistence by the Chief Burbach and the Po-

OPENING OF NEW FIRE STATION
WEST ALLIS OCT. 4-1930

lice and Fire Commission, a new fire station was finally built. The department moved into their new quarters and commemorated the accomplishment with a grand opening on October 4, 1930.

Chief Burbach Dies

Peter H. Burbach was a member of the West Allis Fire Department at least since its inception as a volunteer organization on May 9, 1906. He was appointed Chief on February 14, 1907. Chief Burbach guided the department through many early changes including the acquisition of motorized equipment in 1916, the transition into a paid department in 1925, and the construction of a new station in 1930.

Shortly after moving the department into its new quarters in 1930, Chief Burbach became ill with a severe attack of sciatica and was hospitalized for six weeks. He returned home on November 27th 1930, and had recuperated enough to return to work Thursday, December 11th.

He became sick again the following Saturday, and was diagnosed with appendicitis the next Monday. Emergency surgery at St.

In honor of Chief Burbach, the Common Council passed this "Resolution of Condolence" and dedicated Fire Station 1 to his memory

Mary's Hospital in Milwaukee, was unsuccessful and Chief Burbach died on Wednesday, December 17, 1930 at the age of 60.

The West Allis Star reported that funeral services for Chief Burbach were held at 9:00 a.m. on Saturday, December 20th, at Holy Assumption Church, with six members of the fire department serving as pallbearers. His brother, the Reverend Julius H. Burbach officiated the mass.

In remembering Chief Burbach, Mayor Delbert Miller wrote:

> "I regard the death of my friend and Brother Official, Fire Chief Burbach with a feeling of sorrow and personal loss.
>
> "Mr. Burbach has been a man of high character and ability. In his capacity as Fire Chief of the City of West Allis, he was an outstanding character throughout the State of Wisconsin. It is a singular fact that since the incorporation of West Allis, Mr. Burbach has served continuously as Chief of the Fire Department. He organized the original Fire Department about a quarter of a century ago. As head of the Volunteer Department for many years, he gave faithful service at little or no compensation. When the City became of such size that the public safety demanded a full time department, Mr. Burbach recommended the installation of a paid Fire Department, and upon that recommendation, it was so installed.
>
> "The present excellence and efficiency of the Department is a tribute to what has been the great work of Mr. Burbach's life. In giving out this statement I feel that I am expressing the sentiments of every citizen in West Allis who is at all familiar with the

accomplishments of our Fire Chief." – West Allis Star, 12/18/30.

Commissioner Eugene Phalen, of the Board of West Allis Police and Fire Commissioners said:

"It is with a deep sense of personal loss to each Commissioner that we learn of the death of our Fire Chief. Chief Burbach's life's work with the West Allis Fire Department will always be remembered and will stand out in the history of West Allis, as a shining moment to his memory for all time to come.

"His ability and unvarying devotion as a fire fighter for the past quarter has made him outstanding in the State and National Association.

"Personally, I have served under him as a Volunteer Fireman and know of his great work and faithfulness and joy in meeting all of the obligations of life.

"Our sympathy goes forth to his family in their bereavement." – West Allis Star, 12/18/30.

Edwin Bryant Appointed Fire Chief

On December 26, 1930, Edwin Bryant was sworn in as the third Chief of the West Allis Fire Department. Chief Bryant had been an Assistant Chief under Chief Burbach and had been a member of the fire department since 1906.

Chief Bryant's first official act in his new role was to issue a warning against false fire alarms. False alarms were beginning to create a problem for the department, and "practical jokes" had caused recent injuries to

Chief Edwin Bryant and members of the West Allis Fire Department in the 1930's

A fire near south 60th Street and the Northwestern Railroad tracks took three days to control in January of 1932

Images from Station 1

For 25 Years, the West Allis Fire Department had only one fire station. These are some images from the early days of our department

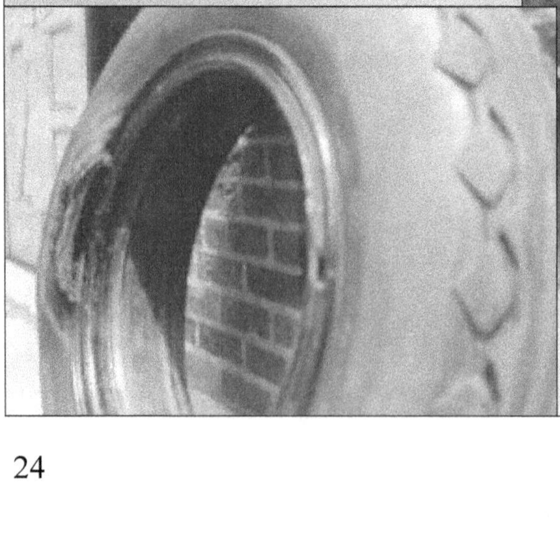

24

25

June 17, 1937
Fire fighters pose with the construction equipment that is ready to begin work on the City's new Police Station at S. 73rd St. & W. National Ave. The building that originally housed the Police and Fire Departments, City Hall and the School Board, built in 1906, had been torn down to make way for the project. The Police have since moved, and this is the site of the present fire station 1, opened in July, 2002.

L to R: Russell Fischer, Leslie Barden, Walter Steffen, William Pohlman, August Marz, William Hayes, George Burbach, Edward Zyniel, Michael Burns and John Petrich, Sr.

On May 7, 1939, fire destroyed the Wisconsin State Fair Park fire station. A new masonry structure soon replaced the wooden barn, and West Allis fire fighters provided fire protection during the Fair from the station until 1991.

firefighters responding to alarms.

First Master Mechanic Dies

Charles Clunie was one of the first members of the fire department to be paid for services rendered. He was hired on March 25th, 1916 as a pipeman and became the department's first Master Mechanic on August 16th, 1924 shortly after the delivery of the first ladder truck. With two pieces of motorized apparatus, a Master Mechanic had become a necessity.

When the City built it's new fire station in 1929, it included a modern mechanical shop for maintenance of motorized equipment.

Clunie held the Master Mechanic position until he died suddenly at the fire station, at 12:02 a.m. on June 17, 1934. His fellow fire fighters served as pall bearers and a fire engine carried flowers for the procession.

Fire Station / Police Station / Alarm Building Plans Change

When Fire Station 1 was built in 1929, it was designed to be the first segment of a three-part process. The entire complex was to be comprised of a fire station, police station and police and fire alarm system building. Political disputes and financial difficulties forced the cancellation of the other two units of the original plan. Finally, in 1937, work was begun on a police station that was significantly different than originally planned, but long overdue in it's necessity.

The "alarm system building" was never built, but an alarm-receiving center was included with the police station. The basement of the neighboring fire station served as a battery power site for the telegraphic alarm box system as well as a fallout shelter during world War II and the Cold War.

The site for the police station was selected to be the site of the original City Hall (at today's 7300 block of W. National Avenue.). The building was built in 1906 and had been razed when City Hall moved to a new site near the intersection of today's S. 70th Street and W. Greenfield Avenue.

Emergency Medical Services

The West Allis Fire Department adapted to changes in a growing community by learning how to provide a variety of services. As early as the 1930's, firefighters worked with police officers to respond to life-threatening emergencies. Firefighters provided first aid and medical care, while police officers transported the sick and injured, most often with a firefighter on board. Early attempts to resuscitate victims seem crude by today's standards, but the work of these caregivers helped shape modern prehospital care.

In 1941, the department purchased a heavy rescue unit that carried equipment to enhance rescue and first aid efforts. Although it carried equipment that was vital to lifesaving efforts, the vehicle was referred to as "the Piewagon" because it's appearance was unusual in American firehouses.

Civil Defense

The fire department encouraged residents of the community to participate in the Civil Defense program as block watch captains and as emergency responders. The department held training drills and organized Civil

Early emergency medical service providers practicing their skills and showing the tools of their trade on the maintenance bay at the fire station in the late 1930's

5001 W. Burnham Street

June 5, 1939

Fire heavily damages a residence near S. 87th Street and West Harrison Avenue

May 11, 1939

5001 W. Burnham Street

June 5, 1939

1942 (above) Mayor Del Miller is photographed with a Civil Defense siren

1943 (left and below) Civil Defense Workers with FD members at Fire Station 1

Defense workers. In addition, the fire station's basement was identified and a fallout shelter to protect residents from a possible atomic attack during the cold war. Long term storage provisions included crackers and canned water. The shelter also had a large supply of radiological meters and backup communication systems as well. The fire department was a distribution point for residential fallout shelter plans that could be built in any residential back yard.

Early versions of firefighter training manuals contained instructions for the evacuation of members to surrounding communities like Wales, WI in the event of an attack. West Allis was identified as a likely location for a nuclear attack because of the local industries that contributed to US defense efforts. The civil defense fallout shelter was regulary inventoried and maintained by fire department personnel until the late 1980's.

Annexation and Growth

In the early 1950's, City leaders began to explore the opportunity of expanding the City's boundaries through the annexation of neighboring towns. The Towns of Greenfield and Wauwatosa, west of the City were attrac-

tive because they offered not only industrial property, but also land that could be developed into homes.

The area of the City doubled in size, and with so much potential for growth, Fire Chief Henry Nelson urged City leaders to increase the staffing of the fire department. He also suggested that new fire stations be built to keep response times reasonable and he laid out a plan for purchasing new apparatus and equipment. His suggestions were heard by City Hall and the department hired 25 fire-

Mayor Arnold Klentz and Fire Chief Edwin Bryant examine a fire truck made by members of the department for distribution to local orphanages at Christmas in 1945

None should be surprised that fire ladders predominate in this large batch of toys because they were made by firemen of the West Allis department for distribution in orphanages at Christmas. A fancy fire truck was examined by Chief Edwin Bryant (right) and Mayor Arnold Klentz while the builders glowed with pride. One hundred fifty toys were made.
—Journal Staff

Training and preparedness have been a fundamental part of fire department activities for years. In these photos from the early 1950's, firefighters train with their apparatus and equipment on S. 74th Street, outside the firehouse.

West Allis officially became a Village in 1902. These scenes are from a parade celebrating the 50 year anniversary of the village in 1952

More parade photos show firefighters in dress uniform marching in step.

Dinner time at the fire house, February, 1947. These photos were taken after a day of record snowfall. Note the snow outside the kitchen window that was several feet deep. These firefighters remained on duty for three days because of city-wide trouble with snow removal.

Photos courtesy Ed Liska, (far right, above)

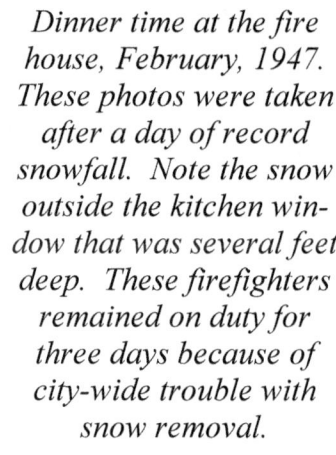
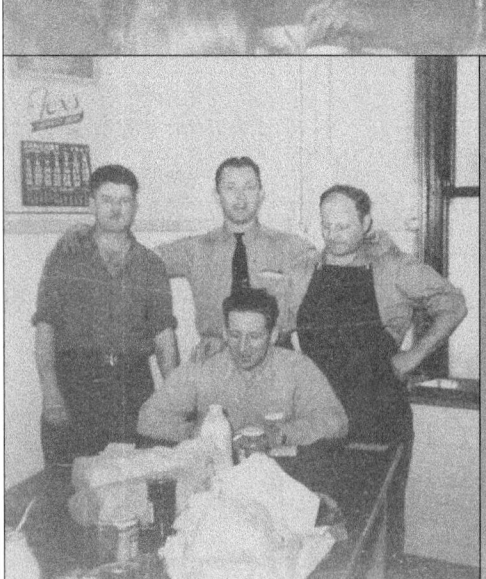

This photo, taken April 26, 1954, shows sixteen firefighters who were hired as a result of City expansion in the early 1950's. They are:
Row 1: Wayne Viel, Bob Mantey, Darrol Ottow, Ken Hoerres, Don Duchow, Smokey
Row 2: Bill Gavigan, Gordy Armstrong, Bob Sabow, Bill Dingel, Mel Yonker
Row 3: John Berens, Don Minturn, Bruce Leifer, Audie Potzner, Ed Zepezauer, Bob Klug
Far right: City Clerk Phil Elliot, Chief Henry Nelson

fighters in 1954 and 22 more in 1955. In these same years, the department purchased two engines, one ladder truck and two water tankers.

Firefighters moved into a temporary fire station just off State Highway 100, south of Greenfield Avenue in 1954 which was called "Fire Station 2" until the current Station 2 at 2040 S. 67th Street was finished and occupied in late 1954. New Fire Station 3, at 10830 W. Lapham Street was completed and occupied in late 1955.

Dispatching Fire Companies

For most of the department' history, telephone calls for service were received by Police dispatchers and transferred to a fire department dispatcher who sent firefighters on their way. This transfer was either through an intercom or by telephone. In addition, an ADT Telegraph receiver in the fire department dispatch center signaled automatic fire alarms. A modern dispatch center was included in Fire Station 2 when it was built was built in 1954 and all dispatchers and receiving equipment moved to Station 2.

To help citizens notify the department quickly, a system of fire alarm call boxes were installed in 1966. The boxes were rented from the Wisconsin Telephone Company. About 140 boxes were located at vari-

Chief John Morch and Dispatcher Les Barden

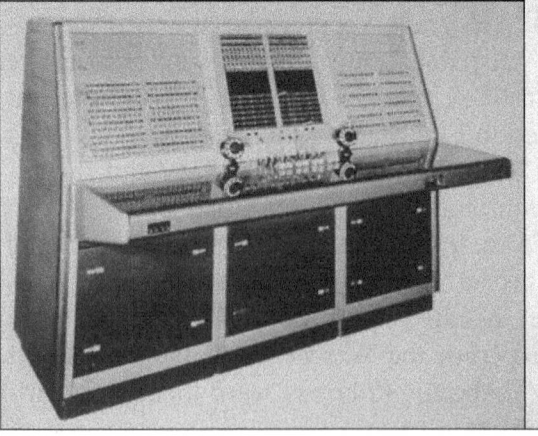

Call Boxes to Be Removed

West Allis — Those funny little boxes scattered around the city and intended to be used for fire emergencies will no longer be in service after Thursday.

The Common Council recently approved a resolution to remove all of the about 140 boxes that were part of the city's emergency reporting system. The boxes were rented by the city from the Wisconsin Telephone Co.

"The costs were just getting too prohibitive from what we were being provided," Fire Chief Robert M. Block said.

Block said a survey of the use of the emergency reporting boxes showed that 89 of the boxes had been used five or fewer times since all the boxes were installed in March 1966.

ous intersections, near the entrances of schools and other public buildings, near high school public pools and in other high-visibility places. Since maintenance costs were prohibitively high and the boxes were seldom used, most were removed in 1978. The city continued to maintain the call boxes near local high school pools until the mid 1980's, when the last of the City's public call boxes were removed.

Bureau of Maintenance and Repair

The department's Bureau of Maintenance and Repair was responsible for the care of all apparatus, machinery and equipment from 1916 until 2002. The bureau was staffed by mechanically-inclined members who were firefighters first, and mechanics second. The City benefited from these dual-role talented individuals to keep costs down while assuring that equipment was ready for use.

Firefighters who worked in the department's Bureau of Maintenance and Repair over it's 86-year history can be proud of their numerous contributions. Evidence of some of the BMR's accomplishments can be seen in the Apparatus section of this book.

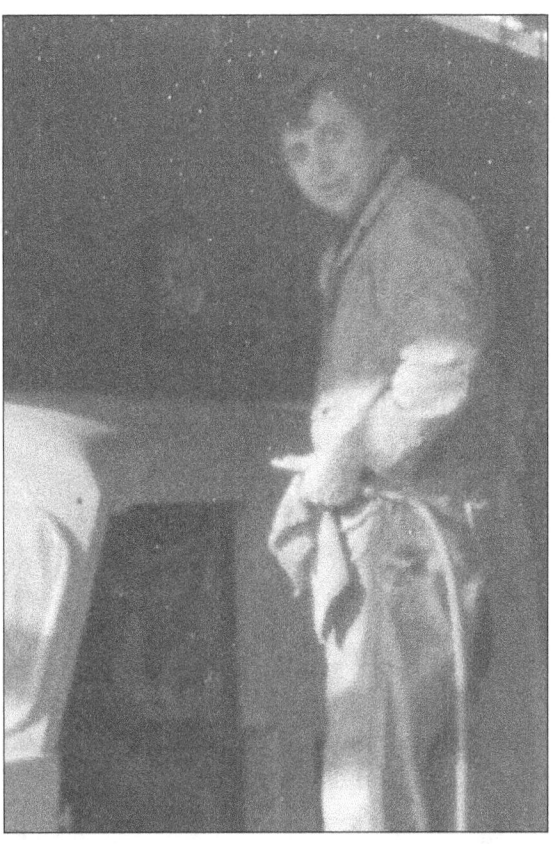

Members of the BMR also accomplished some rather complex tasks. They replaced the open cabs of two trucks with semi-closed cabs that provided firefighters greater protection from the weather. In the mid 1980's, BMR personnel built a service truck that transported a complete compliment of ground ladders and a 25,000-watt generator.

Ten years later, the service truck was replaced by another BMR project. An International Harvester chassis was fitted with a series of compartments, a 25,000-watt generator and a light-duty crane. The unit became the department's tow vehicle for hazardous materials supplies that are used by members of the technical rescue team. The generator on this truck was used to light exit pathways during a power outage at a busy night during the Wisconsin State Fair in August of 2003.

In 1994, BMR personnel renovated a government-owned 1978 Revcon recreational vehicle into a command post for use at a variety of emergencies.

The officer-in-charge of the BMR was responsible for writing purchasing specs for all department apparatus and for procuring virtually all equipment used by members of the department.

After 86 years of service, the BMR was discontinued and maintenance responsibility was transferred to the Department of Public Works' fleet maintenance program. The transfer resulted from increasing pressure to have vehicle maintenance performed by certified mechanics in a risk management effort.

The department will long be grateful to the many personnel who contributed to helping the Bureau of Maintenance and Repair with its many successes over the years.

West Allis Industrial Fire Brigade

As the City's industrial base continued to

grow, the fire department recognized the need to assure that the huge buildings dotting the landscape were protected, and that the people working in them were safe. Although firefighters could get on scene quickly, locating emergencies and getting equipment to them took valuable time.

The Industrial Fire Brigade helped address many of these problems. Most companies had employees that regularly attended training sessions put on by the Bureau of Instruction and Training. The fire brigade had its West Allis roots at the Allis Chalmers Corporation, from which the early Village of West Allis Fire Department was formed at the turn of the century.

The West Allis Industrial Fire Brigade was very active in the community and served as a model for many other brigades. Local industries enjoyed fire losses that were far below the national averages.

The Milwaukee Journal, photos by Dick Graf

Firemen and policemen worked feverishly for more than one and one-half hours Saturday afternoon to free 15-year-old George Rader, of 1337 S. 106th st., after the youth have been caught in the gears of a bulldozer in a freak accident at S. 96th near W. Lincoln. Rader suffered a bruised leg in the accident. *Photo by Dick Gray*

Fire Brigade Gets Award October 7, 1954

The West Allis Industrial Fire Brigade was the recipient of an award for outstanding service Sunday morning. The award was given by the Sunday Morning Breakfast club at the American Serb Memorial hall. Looking over the framed certificate above are (l. to r.) Fire Chief Henry Nelson, Raymond Buettner, vice-president of the Brigade; Capt. August Marz of the fire department; Joseph Fibeger, program chairman of the Breakfast club, and Judge Robert Hansen, principal speaker at the ceremonies. Buettner accepted the award in behalf of Ralph Rheingans, president, who was unable to be present.

STAR Photo

The Industrial Fire Brigade was discontinued in the mid-1980's because of fire department staffing shortages and increased costs. Some business continue to operate in-house fire and emergency responders who seek advice from the fire department's Training and Fire Prevention Bureaus.

Fire Prevention, Inspection and Code Enforcement

The Fire Prevention Bureau was established immediately after the organization of the paid department. Since dues from insurance underwriters were helping fund Wisconsin fire departments, they were required to inspect businesses within their jurisdictions.

As state and local fire codes were getting

This 1968 training session of the West Allis Industrial Fire Brigade was held in the vacant land just west of the Kearney & Trecker Corporation (presently occupied by Quad Graphic's West Allis plant on W. Theo Trecker Drive at approximately S. 112th Street)

An aggressive fire inspection program is the cornerstone of a department dedicated to protecting life and limiting property loss due to fire. Members of the West Allis Fire Department's Fire Prevention Bureau work diligently toward that end. Not only do they routinely inspect businesses of all sizes and multifamily dwellings, but they also assure code compliance to temporary displays and exhibits, as well as new construction, building plans and even fuel storage tanks and facilities.

tougher, Chief Edwin Bryant took a special interest in assuring that these codes were enforced. Chief Bryant was responsible for building the Fire Prevention Bureau into a significant part of the department in the 1930's. Bryant urged the introduction of local fire codes that not only affected businesses and multifamily dwellings but even imposed traffic restrictions that allowed emergency vehicles.

With the goal of compliance as opposed to punishment, fire inspectors have worked hard to maintain a good working relationship with businesses and citizens of the City.

Over the years, the fire prevention bureau has been called upon to inspect all local businesses and multifamily dwellings that contain more than three units. They inspect schools and other public assembly places. They are on scene for fireworks displays, special events, car shows and other programs. Inspectors review construction plans for exit routes, room capacities, extinguishing systems and other safety issues. They have also accepted the task of inspecting and recording

fuel storage tank removals and installations. Fire inspectors also approve all new buildings prior to occupancy. They even assure that Christmas tree sales locations are safe.

Fire Prevention Bureau activities and records are audited annually by the Wisconsin Department of Commerce. A successful audit guarantees insurance dues support of approximately $125,000, and confirms that the bureau is working toward its mission for public safety.

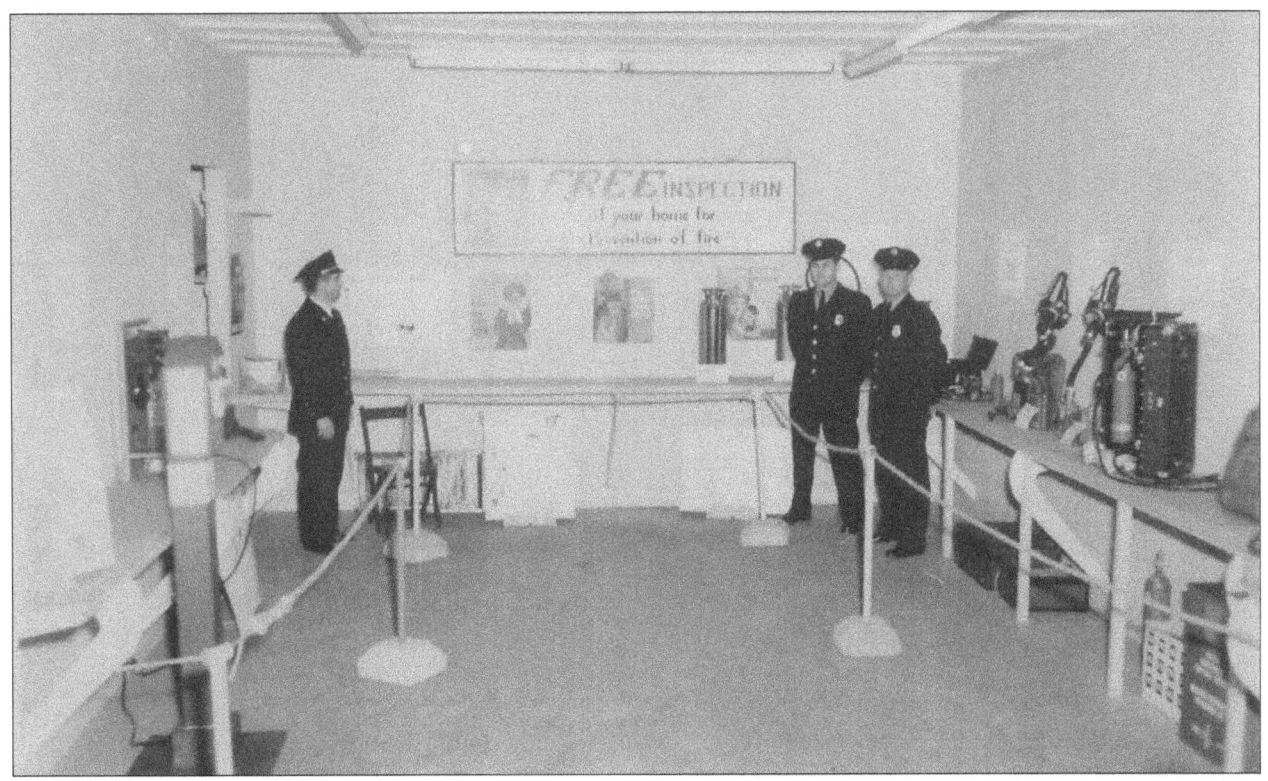

Clarence Lopac, Tony Sparacino and Pat Schimming (1960)

Russ Fischer, John Morch, LT Augy Marz, Laverne Charles and Robert Block (1947)

Bernie Burke, Floyd Strom, Stan Grabowski and CT Chet Newman (1953)

The fire department celebrated fifty years of service with portraits of all members. The photos appear over the next three pages. The officers and staff members are pictured below:

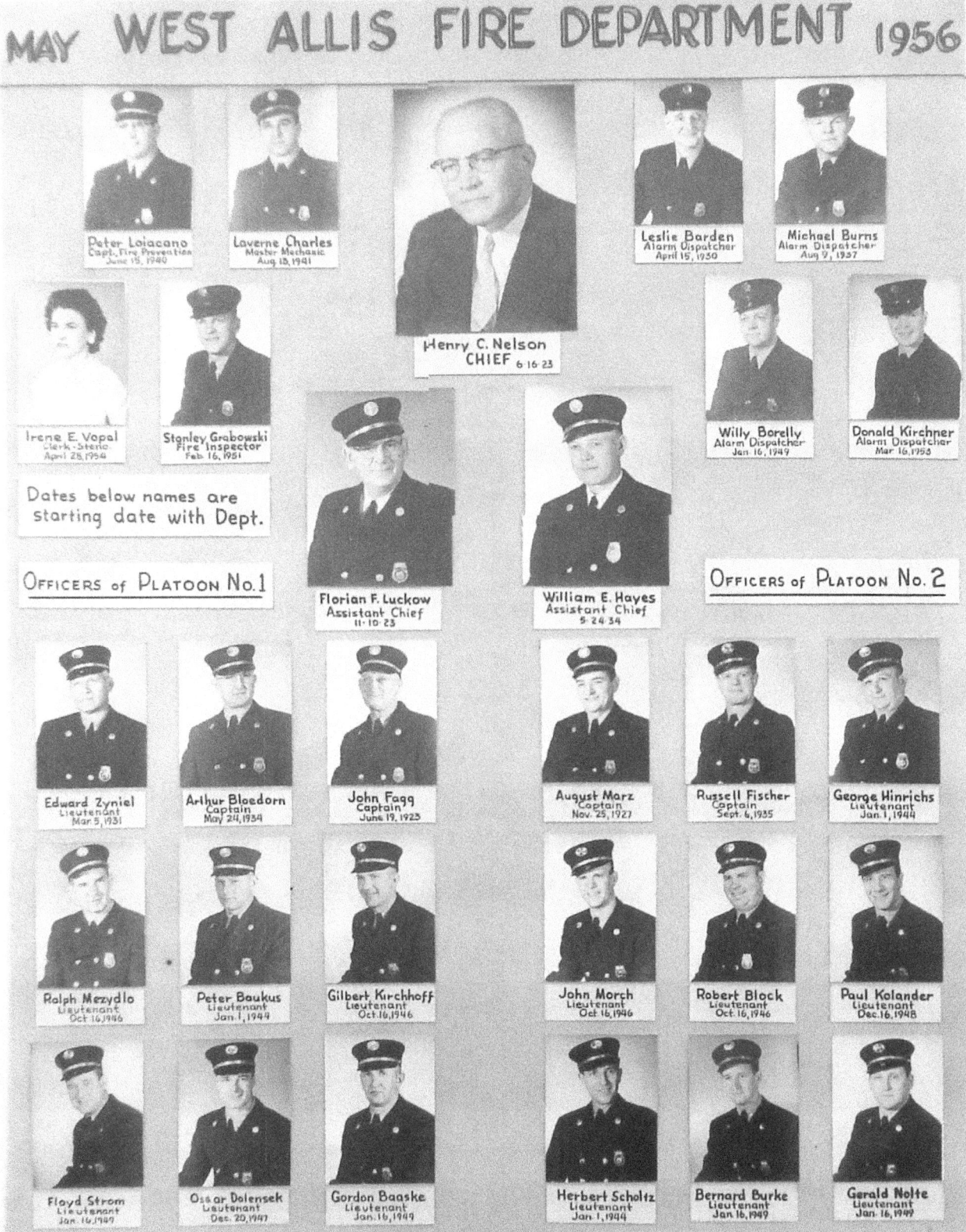

Active Firefighters and Equipment Operators assigned to Platoon No. 1 at the time of the City's 50th anniversary

Active Firefighters and Equipment Operators assigned to Platoon No. 2 at the time of the City's 50th anniversary

Two Major Fires in 30 days
The following pages depict scenes from the Westwood Shopping Center fire of February 20, 1966 and the Burgi's Linoleum fire of March 18, 1966

LT Tony Sparacino and crew work at the Westwood fire

Jerry Kozlik and Joe Horwath work with other firefighters.

Right: Don Debattista and Jim Hughes take a break from cold winter firefighting.

Below: Bill Gavigan looks for hot spots the day after the Westwood Shopping Center fire.

Above: A backdraft knocks Gordon Gleason off his feet, while Don Liedle and another firefighter rush to his aid.

Above: Russ Deakin and Frank Kapitan support a firefighter at the nozzel while working at the Burgi's fire.

Right: Don Debattista and Len Baraga provide first aid for fellow firefighter John Petrich Jr. at the Burgi's fire.

November, 1973
Milwaukee County's First Paramedic Class, WAFD Med 1
Front row: unknown instructor, Ron Barry, unknown instructor, Jerry Breznik, Don Liedel.
Back row: Instructor Tom Olson, Ray Schrader, Bill Beres, Fritz Ambroch, Charles Mellor, instructor Judy Larsen, Darrol Ottow, Clarence Hutto

Paramedics

On November 5, 1973 the West Allis Fire Department's Med 1 went into service as the first paramedic unit in southeastern Wisconsin. With this event, Milwaukee County residents were provided with a dramatic improvement in prehospital emergency care. This new "advanced life support" unit was able to bring the emergency department into the field. Trained firefighters began to administer medication, shock dangerous heart rhythms and treat respiratory problems that previously required immediate transport to the hospital. Paramedics could get advice from physicians over the radio and were able to stabilize life-threatening emergencies prior

Dr. William McManus as "honorary Chief"

to transport, saving lives.

Several Milwaukee area physicians were responsible for beginning the program in Milwaukee County. Drs. John Petersen, William McManus and Joseph Darin had teamed with County Supervisor Richard Nyklewicz and searched for a local fire department willing to accept a significant operational and financial challenge. The group met numerous times with representatives from Milwaukee, Wauwatosa and West Allis to find a department willing to devote the time, money and effort.

Finally, in a meeting at Giuseppe's Pizzeria near Highway 100 and Bluemound Rd. Drs. Darin and McManus discussed the program with West Allis Fire Chief John Morch, and firefighter union representatives Leo Wininger and Jerry Breznik. They outlined a plan for the beginning of the Milwaukee County Paramedic program that placed the first unit in West Allis.

The fire department committed nine firefighters to an extensive training program, provided by medical staff at the County's General Hospital. The lead instructor was a Registered Nurse named Judy Larsen who also wrote much of the curriculum. Doctors Darin, McManus and Petersen assured that the course content was complete. They also provided licensing and medical direction for the future paramedics.

The nine firefighters spent several months in hospital in classrooms and in surgical and clinical settings. West Allis, as a "host community" was required to provide a specialized ambulance that the County helped stock with medical supplies, radios and telemetry equipment.

The first paramedic class in Milwaukee County completed their training and went into service on November 5, 1973. Since then, Med 1 has been joined throughout Milwaukee County by 14 other paramedic transport units and several paramedic engine companies. Paramedics have responded to alarms on motorcycles and bicycles.

In West Allis, paramedics have occasionally used an all-terrain vehicle. The fire department's John Deere "Gator", was specially modified for patient care and transport. The vehicle moves easily through crowds, over rough terrain and across playing fields and parks.

Med 1 and Fire Rescue 2 outside Station 2 in the early 1970's, joined by Drs. Joe Darin and McManus. Med 1's crew is Ray Schrader, Clarence Hutto and Don Liedel. Fire Rescue 2's crew is unknown, Don Valona and Joe Pedersen.

In 1998, West Allis firefighters began serving the community as "paramedic first-responders", delivering advance life support to victims of illness or injury even faster than paramedic transport units. The "PFR" program improved the versatility of paramedics by allowing them to perform functions with less medical direct medical oversight. Fire departments could adjust staffing configurations in order to distribute paramedics across larger areas.

The paramedic program has provided advanced life support in Milwaukee County for over thirty years. Since the program's beginning in West Allis, paramedics have treated over 30,000 people annually and have achieved cardiac arrest save rates that are among the best in the country. The Milwaukee County paramedic program has become a model for similar programs nationwide.

Paramedics with the WAFD "Gator" on a fall afternoon in 2002

Firefighter Paramedics routinely work together with engine, ladder and fire rescue personnel to care for victims of medical emergencies and accidents. At right, a victim is freed from an auto accident for transport to a nearby hospital.

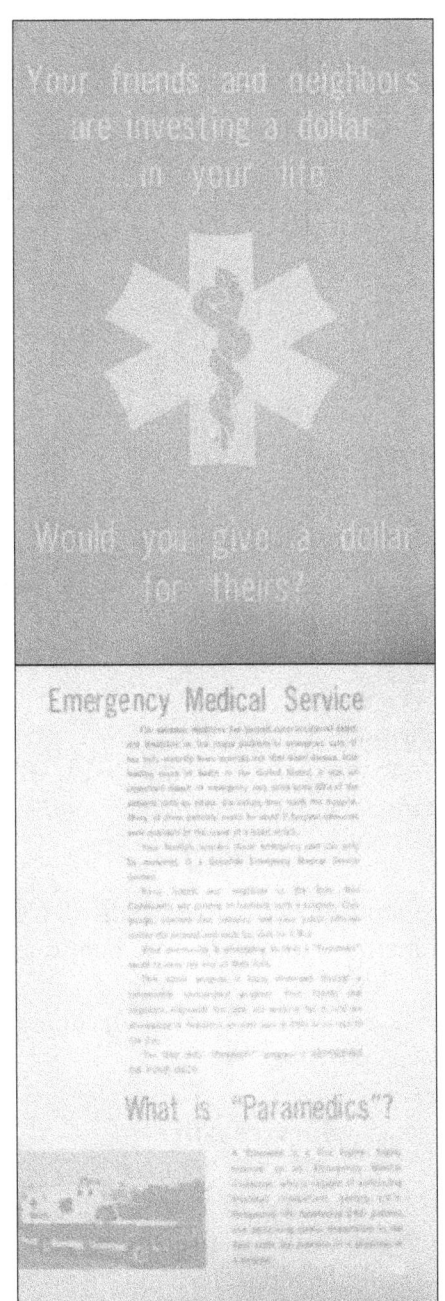

Beginning the paramedic program in Milwaukee County was expensive and required community support. West Allis relied on special groups like the Rotary, Kiwanis, West Allis Charities and others for help. Fliers like the one above as well as a five-part TV documentary increased public awareness and helped rally support. Many individual citizens made donations to help.

A celebration honoring the twentieth anniversary of the Milwaukee County Paramedic Program took place at Serb Hall on November 5th, 1993. The celebration was hosted by West Allis Paramedics and was attended by over 300 supporters, organizers, former patients, media and friends of the program.

In cooperation with the Medical College of Wisconsin, treatments, medications and equipment have been researched here, and have impacted medical protocols across the country.

Survive Alive

In 1983, a group of PTA members and local firefighters visited a fire safety education program in Mishawaka, Indiana. The group, lead by PTA President Judy Cardin, was so impressed by the program that they immediately began efforts to replicate it in West Allis.

The Survive Alive Program is another example of West Allis firefighters working with the community, and special groups to provide a worthwhile program. The West Allis/West Milwaukee et al School District and it's Parent Teacher Association, did most of the legwork in the community. Firefighters made frequent appearances with the PTA to help lend credibility to the fire safety parts of the program. An extensive fundraising effort was coordinated by the PTA and both financial and in-kind donations made the program a success.

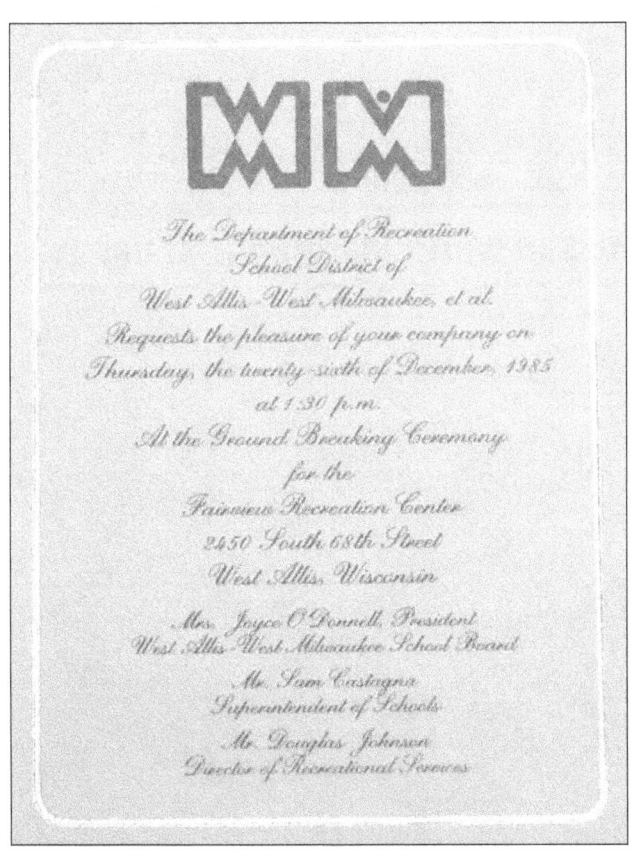

Groundbreaking for the West Allis/West Milwaukee et al School District's new Recreation Department Building housing the Survive Alive Fire Safety House was held on December 26, 1985. The structure was built on the site of the former Fairview School which had been destroyed by fire two years earlier. Each year, 2,500 grade school students learn fire safety practices at the House.

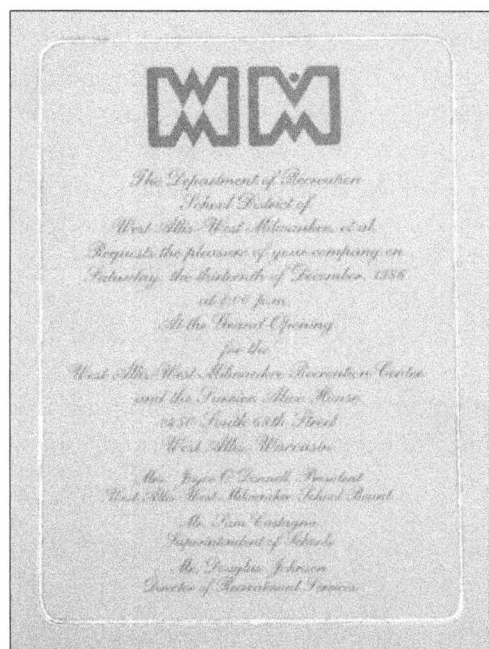

The photo above was taken by a passer-by the night of the Fairview School fire in 1982. The building was replaced by a Recreation Department building housing the Survive Alive House. The Grand Opening of Survive Alive was held on December 13th, 1986.

The Enterprise METRO
Week of September 23-29, 1990
2ND SECTION — Classifieds, Funny Page, Features

Survive Alive experience offers a lesson worth learning first hand

By Barb Falk
Staff Reporter

Stop, drop and roll were the only fire prevention safety tips I can remember from my younger days, but then again I never went through a program as thorough as Survive Alive, a community lifesaving project for children teaching them basic fire safety.

When I contacted the West Allis Fire Department Training Officer Rich Mueller, in regards to a story on the Survive Alive program, he suggested that the best way to get an understanding of the program was to go to the actual Survive Alive house and go through the simulated exercise exactly as the children do.

Arriving at the Survive Alive house in the West Allis-West Milwaukee Recreation Center, 2450 S. 68th St., Officer Mueller led me into a large room. The room had a wooden house constructed against a wall, street sign, street light, benches and phone booth. We entered the house through the front door and walked up a few steps which represented a second floor or the hallway of a one story house.

There were two rooms that the hallway led to, the first room was a control room where volunteer PTA members control the lights and smoke and view children partaking in the simulated exercise through a two-way mirror.

The next room was a child's bedroom. The room had a single bed, a dresser, toys, a rocking chair, closet and three different types of windows.

Officer Mueller explained where not to hide during a fire, opening the closet and pulling up the bedspread to uncover teddy bears that he referred to as "dummies" for hiding. He continued to explain what would take place during the exercise, briefing me on what I should do to escape a fire safely.

I sat on the bed and looked out the windows and the outside of the house was dark. The atmosphere is set for the evening, seeing most fires break out in the night when children are asleep. While sitting on the bed I heard a loud banging noise which was the fire alarm going off. I immediately went to the door, crawling in the proper way, felt the door, it was not hot so I opened it. When I opened the door I was faced with a flashing red strobe light which signaled fire. I closed the door and looked to the windows to escape. Two of the windows had a red flashing strobe light, so I choose the window that did not, unlocking and opening the window I crawled out onto a roof.

While on the roof, I yelled fire and Officer Mueller came up and helped me off the roof. I then went to the pay phone down the street (which is still in the same room) and was instructed to dial 911. upon dialing that number I would have been transferred back to the control room in the house where a PTA volunteer would answer the phone and children would dictate their name and address to the volunteer. After calling 911 children are instructed to gather at a designated meeting place and wait till the firemen or the rest of their family gathers at that spot.

During the exercise I learned several things that I had long forgotten, and in the event of a real fire would have probably panicked and never would have remembered. Throughout the entire exercise a firefighter is with the children in the bedroom, guiding them in the event of something being done wrong. For instance, I wasn't crawling through the bedroom or screaming for help when out on the roof. Also, when the children go through the exercise non-toxic smoke is turned on giving them a more realistic example of an actual fire.

All three of the windows in the room are

See House page M7

The Survive Alive house, located in the West Allis-West Milwaukee Recreation Center, teaches children through a simulated exercise basic fire safety and ways to protect themselves and their families in the event of a fire emergency. Fire Prevention Week is the first week in October.

The "Survive Alive House" was built in 1984 in the new home of the school district's Recreation Department. Ironically, the Rec Department building had replaced the old Fairview School that had been destroyed by fire in 1982.

Survive Alive's first class took place in the spring of 1986. The program has run continuously ever since, throughout the school year. About 2,500 students attend the fire safety education program each year.

The Survive Alive House features a setting with a life-size child's bedroom, hallway, closets, windows and doors. Children visit the house as part of a five-lesson program. Lessons held in their own schools teach fire safety practices that are reinforced when they come to Survive Alive.

At the House, second and sixth-graders have a chance to practice skills like "stop, drop and roll", crawling low in smoke and reporting fires. They participate in a life-like scenario of a real fire in their home.

Students begin their scenario in the Survive Alive bed, as if they are asleep at home. A smoke alarm sounds, and the child escapes from the house safely. Firefighters observe all phases of the exercise and any mistakes are corrected immediately.

The scene ends after children make a safe exit from the House and call the fire department. They even speak with a real dispatcher, over a closed-circuit telephone connection.

The Survive Alive Board of Directors still relies on PTA members for fundraising and teaching help. Community Development Block Grants also support the continuing operation of the House. These funds help minimize costs to public and private schools that attend the fire safety training.

PTA volunteers and West Allis firefighters staff the House for classes which run every Monday and Friday throughout the

Above, fire destroys three buildings on the Wisconsin State Fair rounds in September of 1985. Below, The Milwaukee Journal reports on the destruction of Building G of the Hills Apartment Complex in February of 1982.

Fire destroys John Dewey Junior High School in 1983

Firefighters battle an early morning tavern fire on Greenfield Avenue

Jim Ley Photos

school year. Transportation is provided by the school district and maintenance work on the House is performed by School District staff and fire department volunteers.

Hazardous Materials Level B

In the early 1990's, fire department rescuers were responding to an increasing number of emergencies involving the release of hazardous materials. More and more dangerous

Ice Rescue practice at Quad Graphics, left and below

Firefighters practice their ice rescue techniques at local lagoons. Below, the setting is McCarty Park in early February.

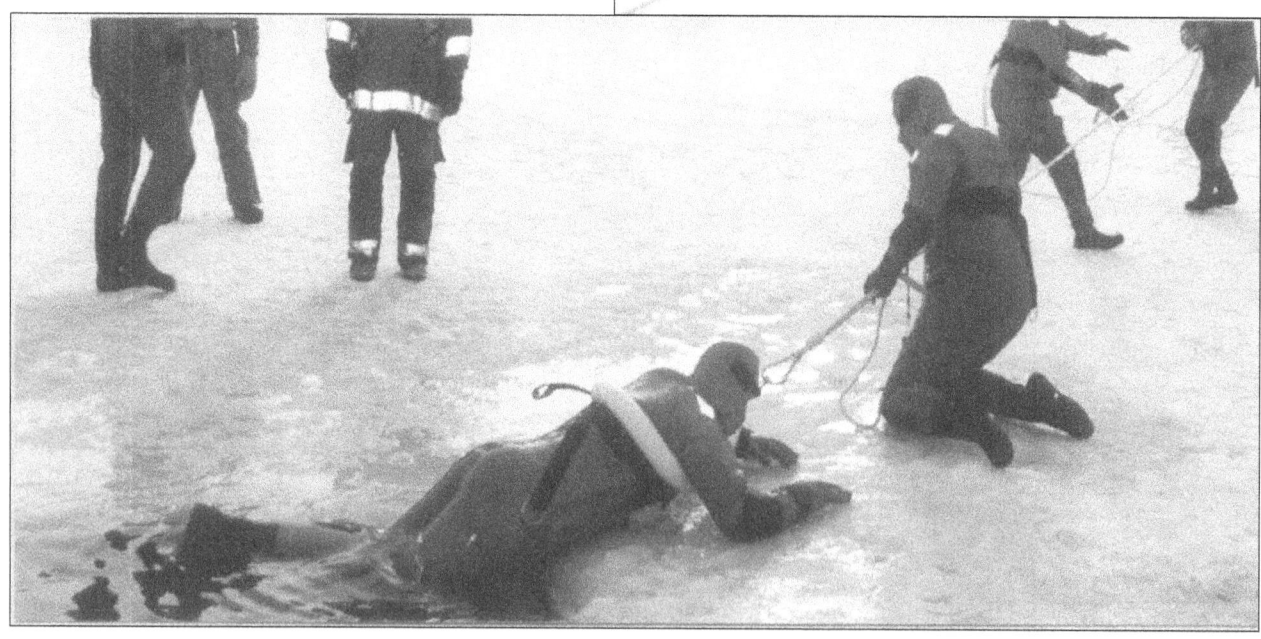

Technical Rescue and Hazardous Materials Level B responses are provided by West Allis Firefighters

In this 1995 photo, firefighters used a vacant manufacturing plant to train on hazardous materials response.

Above, On October 20, 1993, firefighters worked at a polychlorinated biphenyl PCB release at the West Allis Athletic Complex. PCB is a carcinogen that is found in some types of electrical transformer oils.

Confined Space Rescue techniques are essential in a city with industry, transportation and sophisticated water and sewer systems

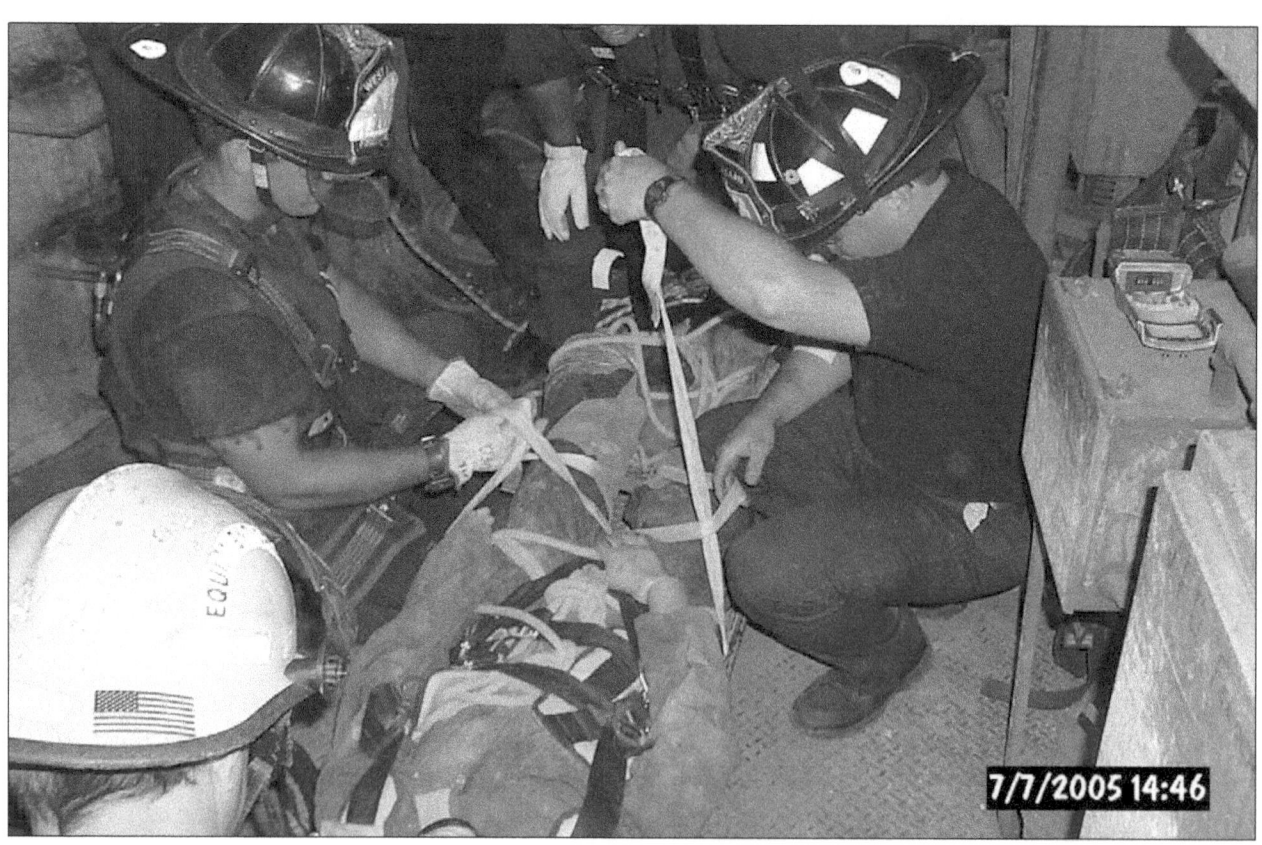

chemicals and materials were being transported across highways, railroads and in air freight. In addition, many more industries were becoming dependant upon chemical processes that could endanger employees and responders if accidents were to occur.

Hazardous materials from uncontrolled disposal or intentional illegal dumping were becoming commonplace in residential parks and vacant property.

In response to these situations and their potential for disaster, the West Allis Fire Department took advantage of training opportunities and federal grants to develop a hazardous materials response team. The team was capable of responding to spills and releases of solid and liquid hazardous materials. This gave them "level B" capability.

The team was limited in their ability to mitigate releases involving hazardous vapors, but could provide rescue efforts until level A responders arrive from the regional team operated by the Milwaukee Fire Department. The regional team is funded by federal resources and is available to any fire department. West Allis firefighters frequently train with the level A team to provide seamless response tactics.

Technical Rescue Team

Shortly after the development of the level B Haz Mat team, West Allis firefighters began preparing for a variety of other challenging emergency situations that required special skills.

In a tunnel rescue incident in 1969, West Allis firefighters prepare to make entry. At left, CT Bernie Burke discusses the operation with Chief John Morch (back to camera) as FF Don Valona looks on. Chief Morch was a strong advocate for tunnel rescue safety regulations and made a significant impact in the safety of local operations.

65

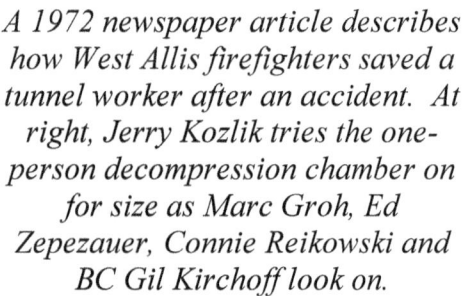
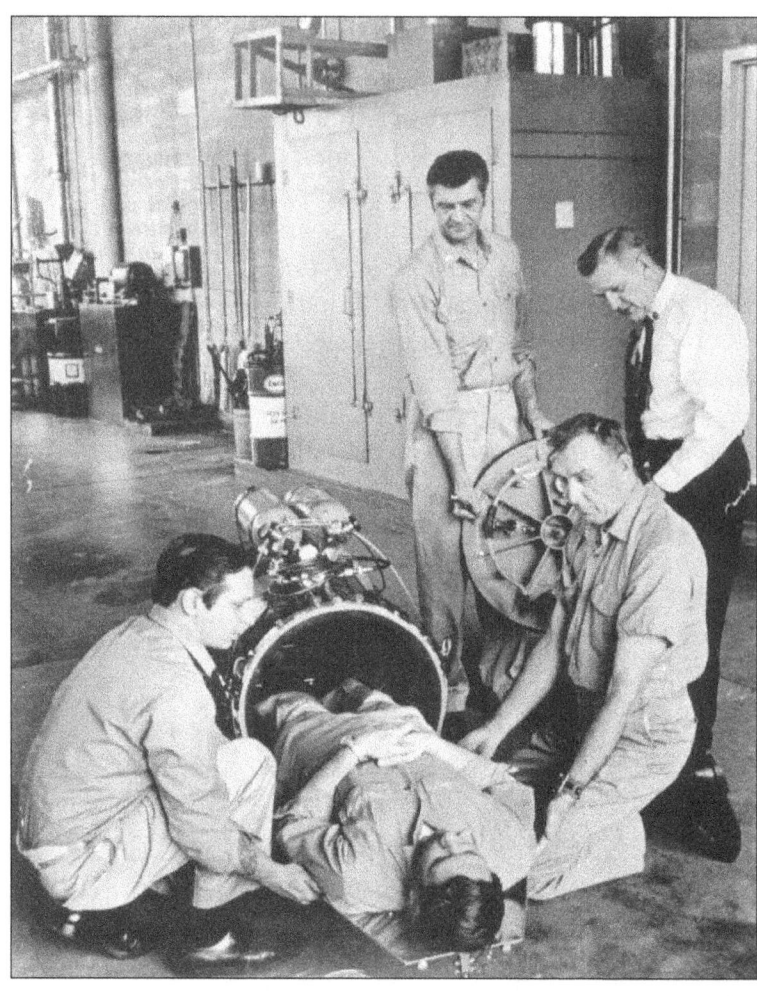

A 1972 newspaper article describes how West Allis firefighters saved a tunnel worker after an accident. At right, Jerry Kozlik tries the one-person decompression chamber on for size as Marc Groh, Ed Zepezauer, Connie Reikowski and BC Gil Kirchoff look on.

The city has two large lagoons in it's county parks as well as an open industrial reservoir and several areas susceptible to flash-floods. The need to develop an ice and water rescue team became apparent as several water and ice-related accidents occurred annually and the potential for a loss-of-life incident was high.

With the many large industrial settings in the city, and with the miles of underground sewer and water system components, confined spaces are common. In the early 1990's, Occupational Safety and Heath Administration (OSHA) regulations were being modified and released. The new regulations prevented employees from working in confined spaces without a rescue team nearby. Confined space rescue capabilities soon became a priority of the fire department.

Finally, firefighters were finding themselves working in unusual circumstances, in awkward angles and at dangerous heights. Although firefighters regularly work in high places using ladders, these situations were different. Rescues from some of the City's industrial settings, from elevated water storage equipment, or in severe weather exceeded the skills of routine fire department responders.

In order to address the special situations encountered in extreme settings, the department added a low-angle rescue component to the Technical Rescue Team. Forty-five firefighters were trained to the required levels of certification to function as TRT members. They could focus on their specialized skills while other firefighters would provide support.

Since September of 1004, the West Allis Fire Department's Tunnel Rescue Team responds to all Milwaukee Metropolitan Sewerage District tunnel contractor accidents in Milwaukee County.

The team has responded to a variety of situations since its inception. Team members also train with other City departments to improve the level of safety that workers and residents of the City can expect. In 2004, the Department of Public Works and the TRT created a trench rescue plan that won statewide recognition as an innovative plan for its efficient use of city resources.

Tunnel Rescue

In 2004, the West Allis Fire Department entered into a contractual relationship with the Milwaukee Metropolitan Sewerage District to provide tunnel rescue services for all MMSD tunnel contractor accidents in Milwaukee County. The Technical Rescue Team accepted this challenge which enables team members to train at MMSD sites. Funding and equipment provided at no cost to city residents, but is the responsibility of MMSD.

Tunnel Rescue Team training enhances the skills of West Allis TRT members and improves the services they provide to residents. In addition, the city benefits from the financial commitment to support the team.

Tunnel rescue is not new to West Allis firefighters. In the 1960's and 70's, tunnel and trench projects throughout the city endangered many workers. Firefighters responded to a variety of accidents including several fatalities.

The tunnel team uses sophisticated equipment and works under very restrictive safety regulations. Lessons learned over the years

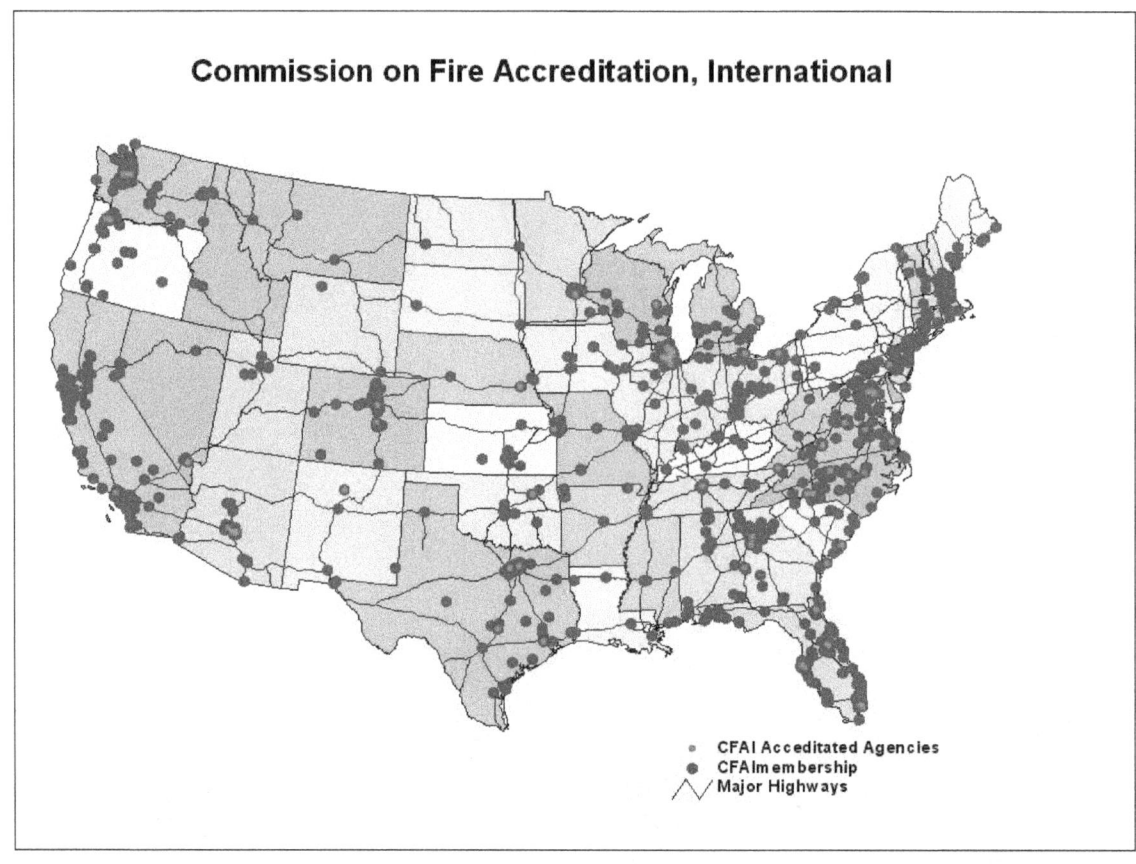

This map shows the locations of fire departments nationwide who are at various stages in their quest for fire department accreditation. Blue dots identify Accreditation Commission members while the red dots identify Accredited agencies. The West Allis FD was awarded accreditation in August of 2003.

have benefited today's rescuers.

International Accreditation

In the spring of 1999, the Board of Police and Fire Commissioners requested that the police and fire departments pursue accreditation for their agencies. The fire department entered the process by becoming a registered agency with the Commission on Fire Accreditation International, Inc. (CFAI). CFAI evaluates fire agencies worldwide to determine whether they meet certain predetermined criteria. CFAI follows a rigorous process in determining whether a fire service agency uses contemporary management techniques and conforms to nationally and locally recognized standards to qualify for accreditation. Over 250 fire service performance indicators are evaluated in this process.

Over a four year period, all departmental policies and procedures were written and updated, a 5-year master plan was created and approved, Risk Hazard and Value Evaluation (RHAVE) data was compiled and studied, and a departmental self-assessment was performed. A "Standards of Coverage" document was developed and approved by the Police and Fire Commission.

The accreditation process culminated in a site visit by a peer assessment group that was responsible for recommending that accreditation be awarded, deferred or denied. They evaluated all written documentation, workplace practices, facilities, apparatus, equipment, training, planning and resource availability. They visited fire stations and interviewed all levels of personnel.

At the conclusion of their visit, the Peer Assessors met with fire department staff members, Police and Fire Commissioners and the City Administrative Officer at the conclusion of their visit to provide preliminary results that were submitted to the Board of the CFAI.

The fire department was awarded accreditation at the August, 2003 meeting of the International Association of Fire Chiefs in Dallas, Texas. International Accreditation reflects directly on the professionalism of all members of the fire department, and confirms that the department meets criteria that support fire service excellence, enhance risk management techniques and improve organizational effectiveness

Semiautomatic Cardiac Defibrillators

In 1993, the scope of practice of Emergency Medical Technicians in Wisconsin was expanded to allow EMTs to defibrillate cer-

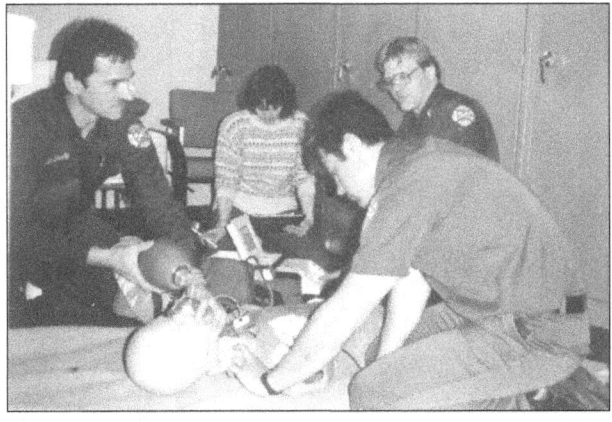

tain life-threatening heart rhythms with a new type of semiautomatic cardiac defibrillator.

On September 11, 2002 firefighters remembered the events of one-year earlier when four passenger airliners were hijacked by terrorists. Two planes stuck the World Trade Center in New York, one struck the Pentagon and the last plane was crashed in a farm field in Pennsylvania before it could be flown into the Capitol. Americans vowed to "never forget" the American civilians and firefighters who died that day.

The department determined that our community would benefit from this new skill. Defibrillators cost about $7,000 each, and the department needed at least two of them to serve the needs of the community. A community-wide fundraising event, coupled with several significant donations helped provide the equipment.

The West Allis Charities and the Rotary Club of West Allis donated one defibrillator, and enough private donations were raised to purchase two other semi-automatic defibrillators for the reserve rescue units. Firefighters were quickly trained in the new equipment and medical protocols.

Two hours after they were placed on the rescue units, one was used to defibrillate a woman who had experienced cardiac arrest and had collapsed at work. With help from the paramedics, the woman's condition was stabilized and she recovered after a brief stay in the hospital.

Public-Access Defibrillator Program

American Heart Association studies have shown that a heart attack victim's chances of survival increase dramatically if trained peo-

(Left to right) John Sinclair, IAFC EMS Section Secretary; Rene Mitchell, VP (Out of Hospital Markets), Medtronic Physio-Control; Jon Tremmel, President, Medtronic Physio-Control; Steven Bane, Assistant Chief of EMS, West Allis Fire Department; Randal Albredens, Firefighter, West Allis FD; Steve Hook, Fire Chief, West Allis FD; Ken Riddle, IAFC EMS Section Chair & Deputy Chief, Las Vegas FD.

ple are nearby and have access to the right equipment to administer an electric shock if the victim collapses from cardiac arrest. Although not all heart attack victims suffer cardiac arrest, a significant number of lives can be saved each year by training people to use Automatic External Defibrillators (AEDs) and by placing the defibrillators in places where people gather. In West Allis, the Public Access Defibrillator program was pushed forward by a local resident, Rita Kohls, who had suffered cardiac arrest and had been defibrillated successfully. Ms. Kohls became the spokeswoman for the fire department's program. She convinced the Parent Teacher Association (PTA) to support the program and it took off. Over the course of only two years, AEDs became available in all public schools and in all City-owned buildings in West Allis. In addition, many local businesses bought defibrillators and placed them in prominent location in their facilities. West Allis firefighters trained school employees, city workers and private business employees in the care of a cardiac arrest victim and the proper use of AEDs.

The Public Access Defibrillation program was so successful, that the fire department was recognized by the International Association of Fire Chiefs and the Physio-Control Corporation, at the IAFC Conference in Las Vegas, even though the department was using another AED manufacturer's product. The American Heart Association's newsletter reported the department's accomplishment in the fall of 2003.

Thermal Imaging

In 1998, thermal imaging equipment was becoming available for firefighting. Thermal imagers use variations in temperature to create a visible image of all objects in a room. Subtle temperature differences between objects allow firefighters using the camera to "see" their way around the inside of a structure, even though a zero-visibility environment is visible to the normal eye, even with flashlights or ambient natural lighting.

The department's first thermal imaging cameras cost over $16,000 and were purchased through donations by the West Allis

Charities and the Rotary Club of West Allis and through federal grants. Technological changes have reduced the size of thermal imaging equipment and their prices have dropped to around $3,500. West Allis firefighters now have thermal imaging cameras on all front-line apparatus, enhancing their fire attack and rescue operations.

CPAT (Candidate Physical Ability Test)

Assuring that firefighter candidates have the physical ability to perform job-related tasks became easier in the late 1990's when the International Association of Firefighters and the International Association of Fire Chiefs developed the Candidate Physical Ability Test (CPAT). CPAT is an 8-station physical ability test is preceded by an 8-week orientation and mentoring period. After extensive testing by fire departments across the United States and Canada, CPAT was determined to be free of gender, ethnic or racial bias. The test could be used with confidence by fire departments who wanted to avoid litigation from unfair testing accusations.

Fire departments who use CPAT are required to perform a transportability survey by polling active firefighters, and considering the department's own tools, equipment and operational practices. All of these combine to give candidates a fair opportunity to prove their physical ability to become firefighters.

Physical ability testing can be very expensive, and the cost of administering a test can limit the quality of the testing that a department provides. To address these issues the West Allis Fire Department applied for, and won a Federal Emergency Management Agency (FEMA) Fire Act Grant for a wellness and fitness program that included CPAT testing and equipment.

Once the CPAT equipment was obtained, the department planned a method to administer candidate testing for fire departments and for individuals interested in becoming firefighters. The expenses of running the program were covered by charging a fee for testing candidates. Fees cover equipment replacement and help purchase fitness equipment for the fire stations.

By administering CPAT, the West Allis Fire Department helps improve the fitness of its own firefighters and enables other fire departments to minimize their hiring risks. The cost of testing candidates is reduced, and the quality of fire service testing improves.

Candidates have traveled from California, Colorado, Arizona and Florida to obtain CPAT certification that is accepted by fire departments across the U.S. and Canada.

Solvox Fire Injures 10 Men
Damage Estimated at $11,500

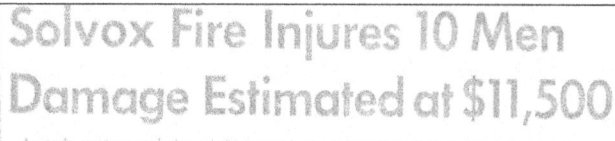

An early morning explosion at the Solvox Manufacturing Co., 11725 W. Fairview Ave., resulted in a blaze which caused an estimated $11,500 damage Monday, May 24.

The fire began in a mixing vat when a metal cleaning detergent was being mixed with sodium hydro sulfide. Either foreign matter or moisture was blamed for the fire, which ignited paper stock above the tank.

Firemen Overcome

Ten West Allis firemen were overcome in the blaze, due to smoke inhalation. One man suffered a back injury when he fell. Six men were sent home as a result.

The fire heated metal drums containing the sulfide and as firemen reached the mezzanine floor the drums exploded knocking firemen off the stairs and showering glass fragments over the area.

Aid Agreement

Due to a county mutual aid agreement firemen from Wauwatosa assisted city firemen at the scene. Wauwatosa sent one engine and an assistant fire chief to the fire.

Fifteen West Allis firemen were called from home to help with the blaze. Some were kept overtime to replace the men who were sent home.

Treated at county hospital were Battalion Chief Arthur Bloedorn, 2234 S. 104th St.; Lt. Arthur Suda, 3725 Cleveland Park Dr.; Lt. Clarence Lopac, 2664 S. 96th St.; Charles Mellor, 826 S. 106th St.; Peter Sparacino, 1533 S. 60th St.; Gilbert Becker, 1630 S. 96th St.; Leo Winninger, 2822 S. 91st St., and Gordon Gleason, 2222-A S. 57th St.

Melted Paint

West Allis Fire Chief John Morch stated that the toxic fumes from the blaze melted the paint from fire engines which were in the street 100 feet from the fire.

He also reported that moisture from the truck enabled the fumes chemicals to settle on the engine and eat away the paint. Morch reported that moisture in the firemen's lungs allowed the chemical to hamper firemen who breathed the fumes. Gas masks were worn but only partly helped.

Keys carried in the firemen's pockets and fittings on the fire truck turned black from the fumes.

Morch reported that all the equipment had been cleaned and was prepared for call. The fire was brought under control after about an hour. Damage was heaviest in the chemical mixing room where the blaze started.

Smoke and chemical fumes engulfed West Allis firemen as they fought a blaze at the Solvox Co., 11725 W. Fairview Ave., Monday, May 24. The fire started in a mixing vat and caused $11,500 damage. Ten firemen were injured in the blaze caused by inhaling the toxic fumes. (Star Photo).

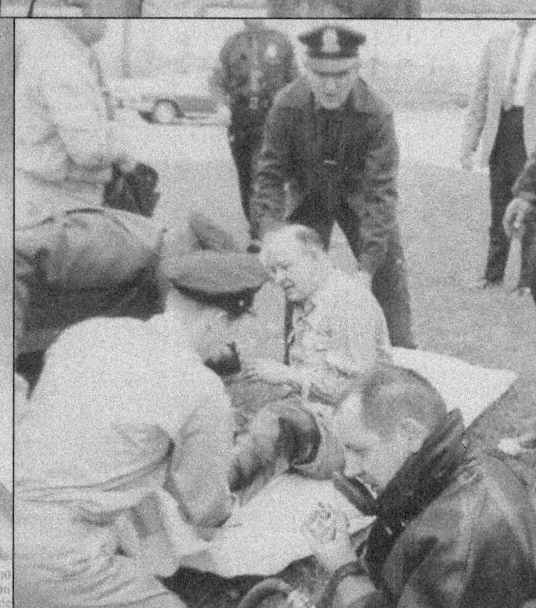

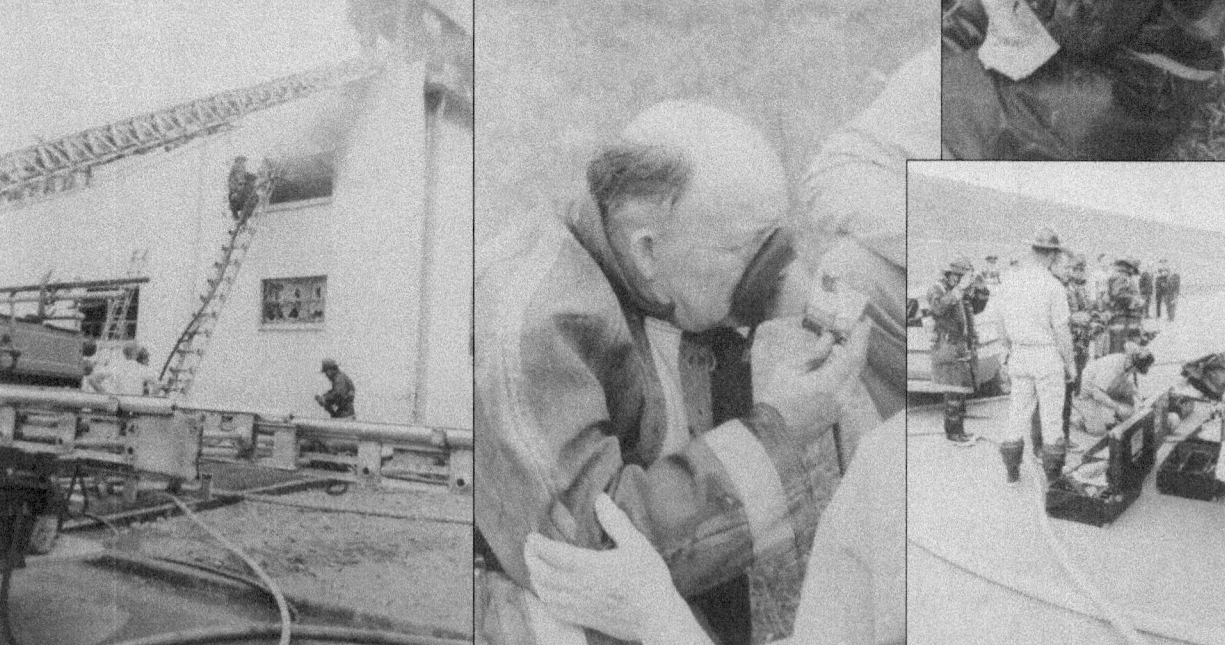

Chapter 3

The Fire Stations

Today, the City of West Allis consists of just over 11 square miles of completely developed suburban residential, commercial and industrial property. The City grew from the businesses that cropped up in the Honey Creek Settlement and neighborhoods around "the five points", where W. Greenfield Avenue, W. National Avenue and S. 62nd Street intersect. The first fire station was placed in the center of the growing community in 1906, and also served as the center of government. When incorporated as a City, West Allis was only about four square miles.

In the mid-1950's, West Allis annexed land west of the city limits that more than doubled its size. Two additional fire stations

The original home of the West Allis Volunteer Fire Department was built in 1906 and housed the fire and police departments, City Hall and the School Board. The horse barn is to the right of the building.

On The Move...
A Timeline of the West Allis Fire Stations

Fire Station No. 1

7332 W. National Avenue

1929: Fire Station No. 1 built, Fire Department moves in from Village Hall next door.

1954: Several fire companies move to Fire Station No. 2

2003: Firefighters move next door into new Fire Station No. 1

2004: Building remodeled into Fire Administration building.

Fire Station No. 3

Temporary site: East side of S. 108th St., 1/4 mi south of W. Greenfield Avenue

1953: Named Fire Station No. 2 (Temporary), Referred to as the "Quonset Hut", replaced by Fire Station No. 3 in 1955

10830 W. National Avenue

1955: Fire Station No. 3 built, firefighters move in from nearby temporary station.

2004: Fire Station No. 3 remodeled, fire companies move back from temporary quarters at Parkway School

Temporary Site: Parkway School, 2930 S. Root River Parkway

2003: Station 3 companies move into temporary station while Fire Station No. 3 is remodeled

Fire Station No. 1

7300 W. National Avenue

1906: Village Hall, Fire Station, Police Station and Jail, School Board

1938: Original building razed, new Police Station built

1994: Police station razed when Police Department moves to 11301 W. Lincoln Ave. (lot becomes vacant)

2003: New Fire Station No. 1 built, firefighters move in from previous Fire Station No. 1

Fire Station No. 2

2040 S. 67th Place

1954: Fire Station No. 2 and Training Site built, many of the firefighters assigned to Station 1 move in.

2005: Fire companies split between Stations 1 & 3 during remodeling of their quarters

2006: Fire Station No. 2 and Training Site remodeled, fire companies move back.

In these photographs, additions to the original building can be seen. A two story section and additional garage space has been added to the north. The barn has disappeared to make way for the new construction. The photo above was taken in 1916, below, in 1925. The building was razed in 1938 to make way for a new police station. By then, City Hall and School Board offices had moved out, and the fire department had moved into a new station right next door.

Fire Station No. 1 was built in 1929, after several years of political debate.

were built and occupied. West Allis firefighters have been providing service to the community from these locations ever since.

Fire Station No. 1
7332 West National Avenue

The city's original fire station, a building which housed the combined services of city government, the school board, the police department and jail had become increasingly crowded as the city grew in the early 1920's.

On July 1, 1926, the West Allis Star reported that the Common Council was considering the purchase of land adjacent to the current building, that was a portion of the Central Improvement Company subdivision. The article said, "According to C. W. Velser, secretary of the fire and police commission, the need for a site for a fire station is imminent. With the city growing swiftly, he said, it is only a matter of a few years before another fire station will be imperative." The Star went on to report that discussions about a new station had been going on for years, but this request was the first "concrete step."

Two weeks later, on July 15th, the Star optimistically reported that plans for the land acquisition were moving along well. The Council's finance committee had entered into negotiations to purchase land and, "...Further evidence that plans for a new station will soon become a reality is seen in the action of Fire Chief Peter H. Burbach and members of the Police and Fire Commission who will make an exhaustive personal observation of various fire stations in other cities." In fact, "...C. W. Velser, Secretary of the Police and Fire Commission, said today that members of that body and the Fire Chief have signified their intentions of making a careful study of fire house stations in other cities at their own expense so as to have an intelligent understanding of the latest and most efficient types

Moving Day Keeps Firemen Busy

West Allis' fire department moved into its new home at Sixty-sixth and National avs. Monday, the entire process taking only a few hours. By noon the job was completed and by 2:00 p. m. the firemen had answered three fire calls. The above photo shows the "clean-up" squad carrying in the last load from the old station. They are (from left to right) Walter Steffen, Joseph Hayes, John Petrie, Harry W. Betzhold, Robert Miller, William F. Beck and Charles Schultz.

of construction."

While the Star reported optimistically, however, behind the scenes trouble was brewing. On October 7, 1926, the Star reported that fire station plans would be delayed. The building under consideration had evolved into a combined Police and Fire headquarters, because both departments were in dire need of space, and time was of the essence. But the building was projected to cost $143,339. In order to fund the project the issuance of bonds would be required. The Star reported that, "The Council, while taking no definite action on the request, made it plain that the bonds would probably not be voted because the School Board had made a previous plea for an issue to build new schools and if this request is granted then the Fire and Police Commission plea must be turned down because the city will then have issued the full quota of bonds permitted under the state law."

Mayor Delbert Miller was also concerned with rising taxes. The Star explained the position of city leaders, "According to Mayor Delbert Miller and other city officials, the plans for floating a bond issue to pay the cost of building just the first unit of the structure cannot be considered until the new tax is made up."

With this action, the fire station project was tabled for nearly two years. On September 13, 1928, the West Allis Star reported, sarcastically, that, " Another of the ancient skeletons, which lie dust-covered in the closet of West Allis' councildom, was dragged forth and then quietly laid back to rest Tuesday night". The Star explained that the Police and Fire Commission had again asked the Council to consider providing a police and

Fire headquarters on the same site requested two years earlier. The Council action was described in detail, "The councilmen rubbed their chins, lingered in thought a while and then with adequate ceremony and solemnity decided that the 1928-1929 budget is not big enough to embrace the building or even the first unit and laid the idea away to be dug up again when somebody thinks of it."

Suddenly, a surprise development. On November 15, 1928, the Star reported stunning news that plans for the first portion of the Police and Fire building was approved by the Common Council. The body had approved $65,000 for the fire station segment of a three-section building that would eventually house the police, fire and alarm service. The article said, "Plans for the proposed city building, prepared by Lindl and Schutte, architects, have been in the hands of the commission for some time and it is almost certain that the plan will be followed....Tuesday night's move by the council came as a complete surprise to the entire city as well as to the commissioners. Building plans that had been laid away for some time, were taken out of their places of hiding today and dusted off for use."

It seemed as if the fire station plan would finally get off the ground. The Police and Fire Commission were poised to approve the plans that they'd had on file for over two years. They were ready to build a three-segment structure, beginning with the fire station, followed by the alarm system building and finally the police station.

Meanwhile, the Commission had plans to remodel the existing 1906 building for the

In the photo above, taken in August of 2002, notice the exterior brick section that was intentionally covered with inexpensive brick veneer, in expectation of the construction of an attached fire alarm communication building. The addition was part of the original plan that was delayed in 1929 because of funding shortages. The addition was never built. Instead, firefighters received alarms through the original telephone and Allis Chalmers steam pipe system until a new police station was built in 1938 that included a telephone dispatch office for all citywide emergency calls.

police department. It seemed as if the project was moving forward; and then...

On January 3, 1929, an editorial ran in the West Allis Star that aroused some interest, and caused some hesitation on the part of several alderman and the Mayor.

The editorial raised the issue of "southside" fire protection. It described how the railroad tracks dividing the city could not be traversed easily. The city already had a fire station on the north side of the tracks, so the editorial offered a solution, "...Instead of spending $65,000, truly a great amount to spend for a station that will not contribute much to the situation, why not split that amount into several parts and build a small unit somewhere on the south side of the city – south of the railroad tracks? That, we think, would be the most logical plan, and would benefit THE ENTIRE CITY....As a matter of fact, West Allis is large enough to make use of a few substations for police use also, instead of 'putting all the apples in one sack'."

Not limited to location alone, the editorial also raised the issue of city excessiveness in design and expense by saying, "Plans and drawings for the new fire station portray a truly imposing building – a building that would be a contribution of beauty and art to any city. Unwise, we call it."

The article caused enough of a stir to delay discussions for another four months, until finally on April 4, 1929 when the Common Council approved the funds for the fire station from the city budget. However, only $50,000 was allotted for the station. The alarm system building would have to wait, or move to City Hall. The Star reported that the "...Common Council Wednesday night passed a resolution instructing M. C. Henika, city clerk, to advertise for bids for the new fire and police station." Again, it seemed as if the project was moving forward; and then...

On May 16, 1929 the Star reported another delay. This time, even though Pfeifer Construction Co., the successful bidder for the contract, was prepared to start excavating, the work was halted because of a bond issue. The Star reported, "...a representative of the bonding company appeared before the city council with a report that may see the indefinite postponement in of the building of the station. Attorneys of that concern returned an unfavorable answer on the city bonds, holding that they could not be offered for sale due to the fact that the Wisconsin statutes do not specifically allow to issue bonds for the building of a fire station. It is their opinion that the issue must be referred to the people through a referendum. They also stated that due to the fact that the bond ordinance was not passed by the city within the sixty day

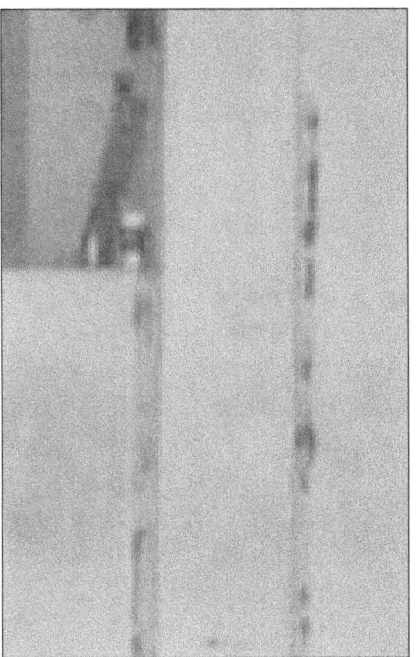

What's a "jezo"?

Fire Station 1 was built in 1929 by local contractor Martin Jezo. Columns in some of the basement walls extended about 1 1/2" out of the walls. When firefighters built a handball court in the basement, these concrete vertical steps were filled by angle-cut wood to decrease the affect of handballs hitting the obstruction. Firefighters called the concrete obstructions "jezos" after the contractor. If a ball hit the jezo, it resulted in a "do-over". If a hand hit the jezo, it resulted in an "injury" and sometimes a broken finger.

Members of the fire department gathered in front of Fire Station No. 1 for this 1954 photograph.

limit from the time of the initial resolution, the bonds could not be offered for sale."

In October of 1929, the city received word that the fire station bond issue was legal. However, bidding on the contract would need to be redone because of the delay and because of the uncertainty created by the bonding. On October 10, 1929, the Star reported, "...So confident was the city in their work, that a contract for the erection of the fire house was granted before the bond issue was returned by the bonding house. Pfeifer Construction Co., low bidders had a steam shovel on the site ready for excavation when word of the refusal was received."

In late November, bids were again opened, and a local contractor, Martin Jezo, was the low bidder and was set to begin work. Again, it seemed as if the project was moving forward; and then...

In yet another controversial development, the West Allis Star reported, "...Throwing a placid, unsuspecting council into a state of chaotic uproar, Mayor Delbert Miller announced alleged irregularities in the opening of contractors bids for the new fire station and ordered a special investigation to be held at city hall....He stated reports had been circulated that some members of the administration had told others the name of the lowest bidder 24 hours before the bids had been opened."

Mayor Miller was also concerned about rumors that had been circulating alleging uncertainties about the surety bond accompanying the low bid, written by the Miller Velser Company, in which he was a partner.

The investigation took place. No improprieties were revealed, and fire station construction <u>finally</u> got underway. The station was finished and occupied in mid 1930.

The building was state-of-the-art for its

Fire Station Remodeling

Fire Station No. 1 was barely 35 years old when talks of remodeling were beginning. And by the late 1970's this type of talk was gaining momentum.

Unfortunately, the late 1970's was the beginning of an economic decline in West Allis. The City was feeling the effects of a nationwide recession. Several large industrial giants were poised to move or close. Allis

Fire Station Repair Called Urgent Need

September 10, 1977
West Allis Star

Fire Chief Wants Station Shut

September 5, 1978
Milwaukee Journal

time, and was based on plans that had been compiled by researching fire stations across the Midwest. The fire department was satisfied that it had a facility that would serve the needs of the community for years to come.

85

Milwaukee Magazine's January, 2001 edition told the story of Wisconsin Energy's disposal of cyanide-soaked wood chips that eventually lead to a settlement that would supply funding dedicated to the remodeling and new construction of fire department buildings in West Allis.

Chalmers Corporation and the Kearney and Trecker Corporation fell to bad markets and a costly labor market. When these companies closed, along with several smaller employers, city resources were challenged. The fire department faced staffing reductions, and fire station repairs were not on the radar screen for City leaders. The City's focus was on new development to improve the tax levy burden, and the fire department's ability to "make do" with existing buildings was tested.

In 1990, a task force was organized to study the feasibility of remodeling or rebuilding police and fire buildings.

The task force suggested that a new police station was required immediately, because of a host of issues related to the safety of the officers, civilian employees and prisoners that were being held in substandard facilities.

The task force also recommended that Fire Station No. 1 be replaced by a more modern facility. They concluded that the building had multiple structural defects, inadequate heating and cooling systems, and an insuffi-

cient electrical system.

The task force felt that the building defects would be too costly to repair, and suggested that the City should consider a new building instead of remodeling.

With the task force's recommendations on file, City leaders approved the construction of a new police station in 1993. When the building was finished, the cost of the police station exceeded its budget, and forced the delay of any fire station plans. The old police station was demolished, leaving a vacant lot next to Fire Station No. 1 for the next nine years.

The "Blue Ooze"

On April 17, 1992, West Allis firefighters were called to a report of a blue liquid oozing from the ground and floating down Underwood Creek. Firefighters contacted the Department of Natural Resources, who worked with the Environmental Protection Agency and Wisconsin Emergency Management teams to identify the liquid. Chemical analysis showed that the mysterious fluid contained a complex form of cyanide. The hazardous site was just north of Theodore Trecker Way near S. 113th Street, on property owned by the City of West Allis and the Giddings and Lewis Corporation.

It was determined that the cyanide was produced as a byproduct of Wisconsin Energy's production of manufactured gas that was used to generate electricity in the 1950's. The cyanide was soaked into wood chips, removed from the manufactured-gas plants, and deposited in West Allis. Eventually, some of this land became Wisconsin Energy's training site. In addition, the tainted wood chips were discovered all along the corridor where the company had built transmission lines. The hazardous waste was used as fill to level the land on the site.

The City sued over the release of this dangerous chemical and won. The court established damages at $104 million, and the Wisconsin Electric Power Company (WEPCO) quickly appealed.

Lawyers for WEPCO, which had since become WE Energies, argued that the penalty was excessive because: 1) they had removed the hazardous waste at their company's expense, 2) no injuries, illnesses or deaths had occurred, and finally, 3) the company no longer performed the process that produced the cyanide.

In a negotiated settlement, WE Energies agreed to pay the City $8.5 million for the remodeling of three fire department buildings, the construction of a new fire station and to cover the City's legal fees.

Remodeling Plans Back on Track

The fire department had been working with City leaders to determine the best course of remodeling and new construction to serve the City. Several plans were considered, one of which even making its way to the Common Council for defeat.

After about two years of discussion, a plan was approved to:

1. Remodel fire station No. 1 into an administrative office building,
2. Build a new Fire Station No. 1 on the site of the old police station (which was the site of the original fire station in 1906, and
3. Remodel Fire Stations Nos. 2 and 3.

The buildings would be expanded to accommodate an increasing amount of fire department equipment and apparatus. They would also become compliant with the Americans with Disabilities Act (ADA) and become gender neutral, since the original fire stations had been built to accommodate only male firefighters. Also, the stations would have central air conditioning and improved heating units.

The first step of the fire department's facilities renovation plan would be the construction of a new firehouse on the site of the former police station. This property, along S. 73rd Street, north of W. National Avenue, was the site of the original West Allis combined Fire Station, Police Station, City Hall and School Board headquarters. The original building was built in 1906 and razed in 1935 to make way for a new police station. The police station was razed in 1995 after the police moved into a new Police/Court Center at 11301 W. Lincoln Avenue.

Groundbreaking for the new Fire Station No. 1 was held on August 5, 2002. Representatives of the City included (l to r) Fire Chief Steven Hook, Mayor Jeannette Bell, Common Council President Paul Murphy and Police and Fire Commission President Wayne Clark.

Another goal of the remodeling and new construction plan was to assure that buildings were low-maintenance and built to last. Improved roofing systems and windows would assure longevity of the weatherproofing systems.

Fire Station No. 1
7300 W. National Avenue

The fire station renovation and remodeling plan called for the construction of a new building on the lot vacated by the Police when they moved to 11301 W. Lincoln Avenue. The lot had been vacant for nine years and the seventy-year-old fire house was being repaired on an "as-absolutely-necessary" basis for the last fifteen years.

Plunkett Raysich Architects were hired, and plans were drawn for a building that would meet the department's operational needs and that would compliment the neighborhood. The architects exceeded the City's expectations with a building that was attractive and functional. The building brought in each of the elements of the surrounding structures, including similar masonry, roofing materials that matched the old fire station, stamped-concrete insets and exterior lighting that enhanced its appearance. The new fire station would be 2-stories because of the small lot size, but would be nearly 40-feet high because of the extra-high ceiling on the apparatus floor.

WB Construction from West Bend was the general contractor. The project was completed on time and within it's $2.1 million budget.

The station won several awards for design and architecture. It received honorable mention in Fire Chief Magazine's Station Design program in 2003, and a golden trowel award by the Wisconsin Masonry Institute.

Fire Station No. 1 was finished in May of 2003, and firefighters occupied it in June.

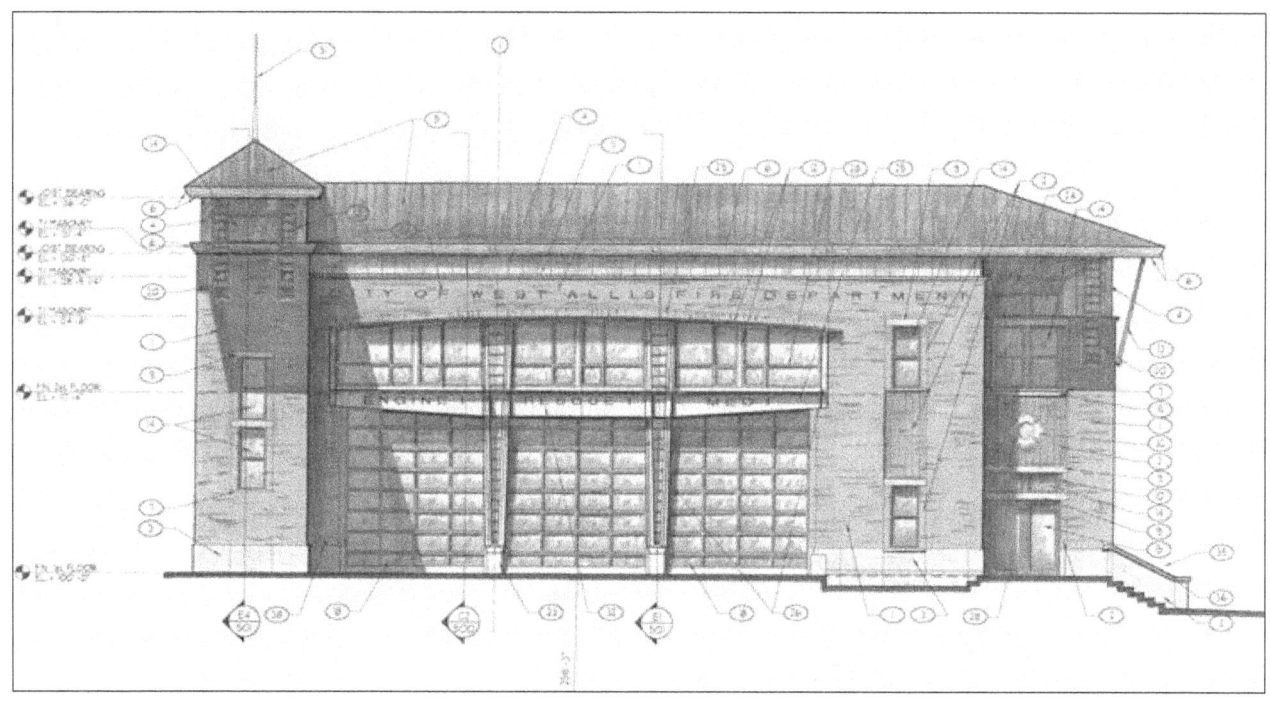

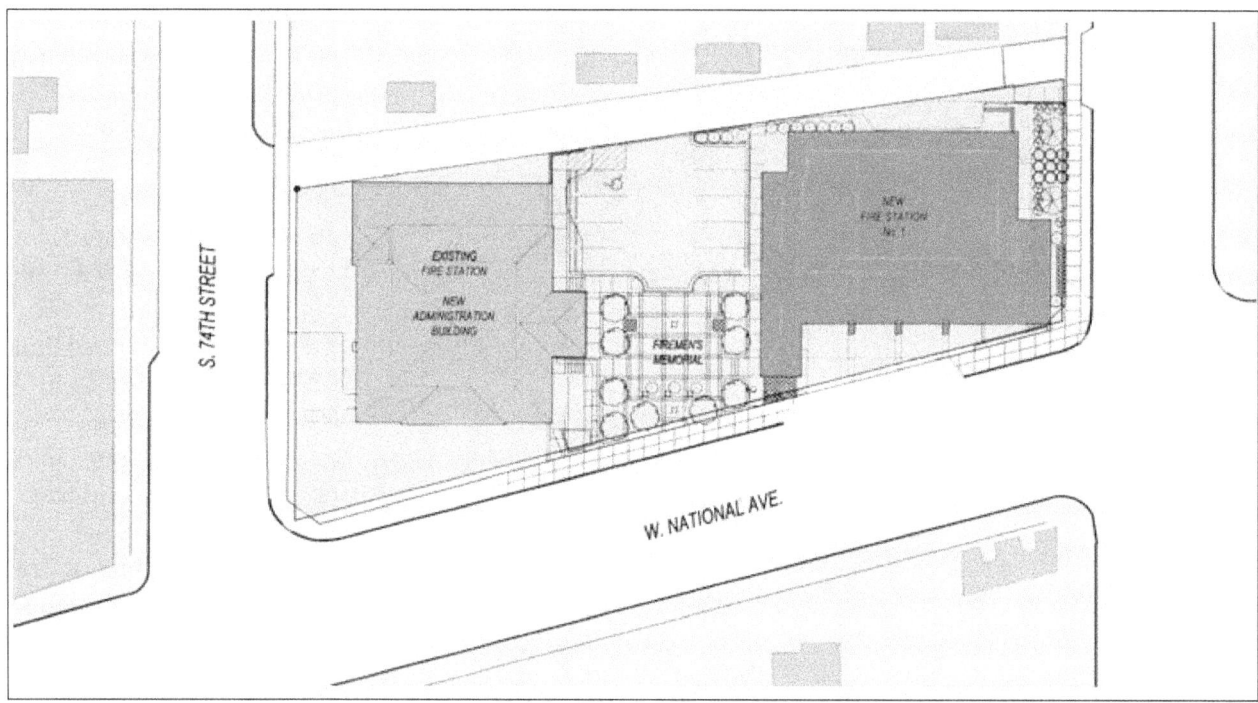

Plunkett Raysich Architects were hired to design all aspects of the fire department facilities plan. The new Fire Station No. 1 was designed to create a smooth transition from the existing fire station (built in 1929) which would remain in place but undergo renovation, and the rest of the neighborhood. The Aurora Clinic to the east and the City's Library across the street were important to the appearance of the entire 7300 block of West National Avenue.

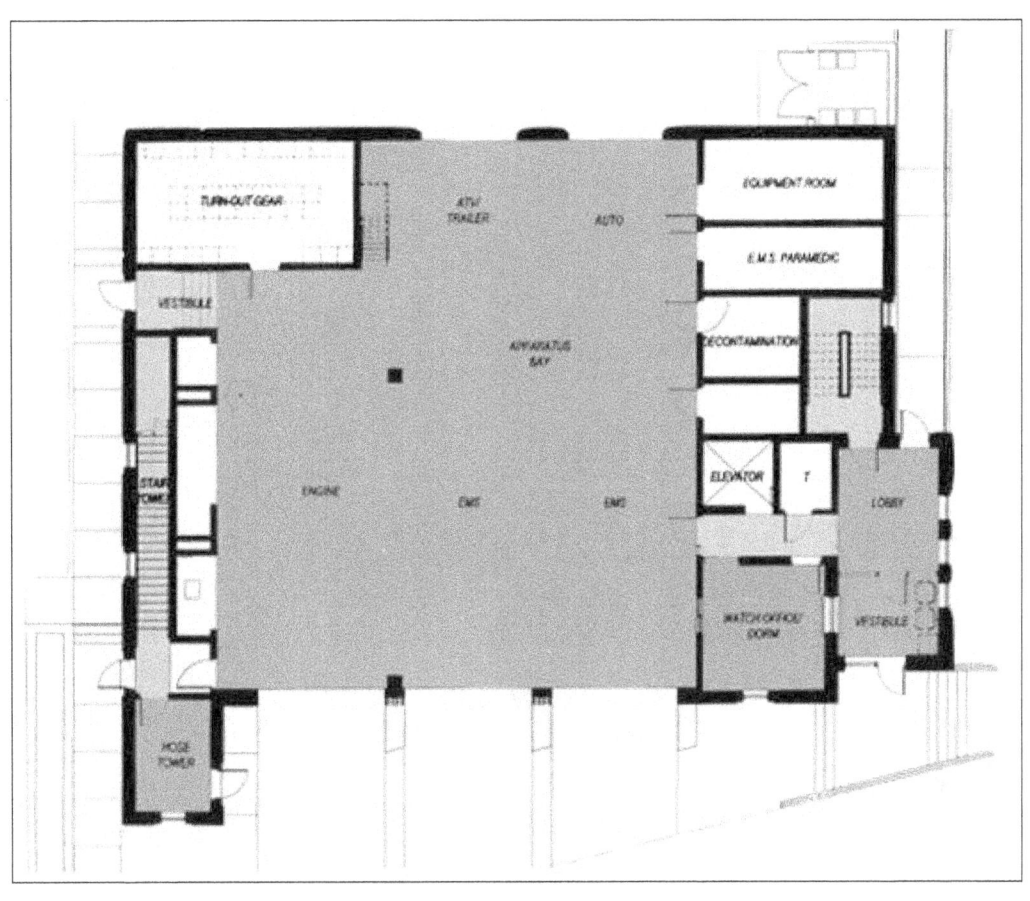

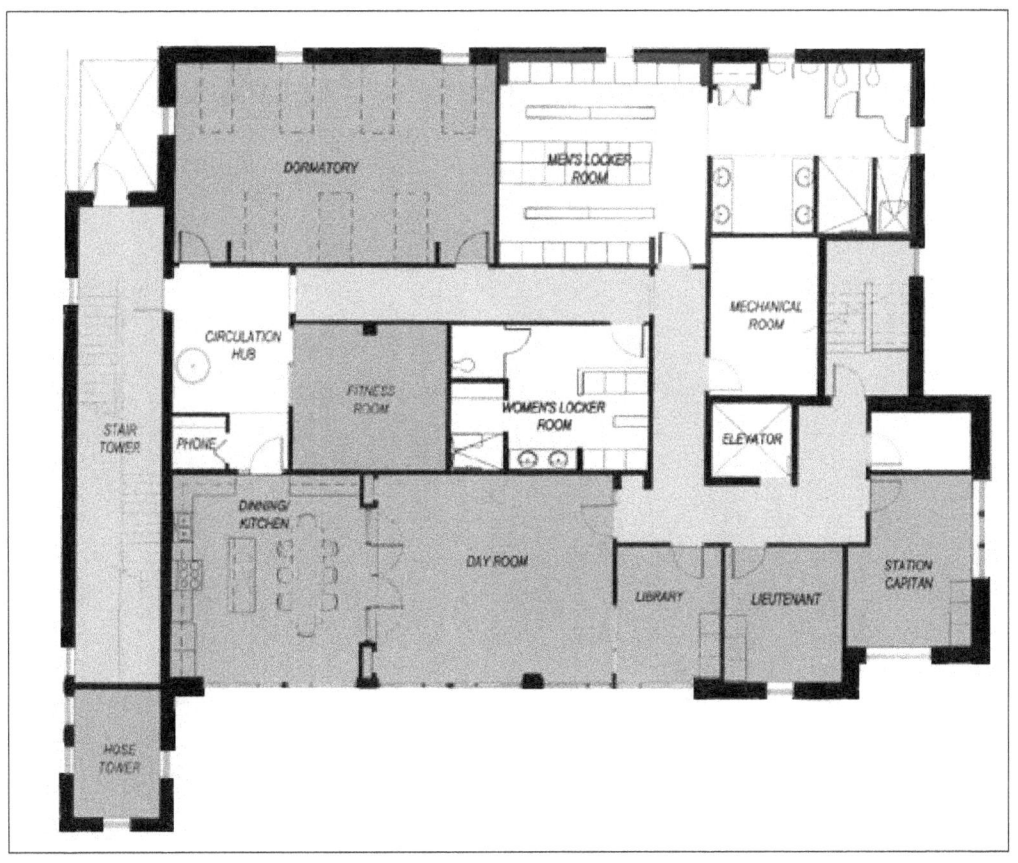

Interior design of the new building was very important. The materials were to be low-maintenance, and energy and spatially efficient. Interior designers worked closely with fire department staff to achieve color and material schemes that could carry through into all fire stations so that furniture and appliances could be interchangeable.

*Fire Station No. 1
Grand Opening
July 26, 2003*

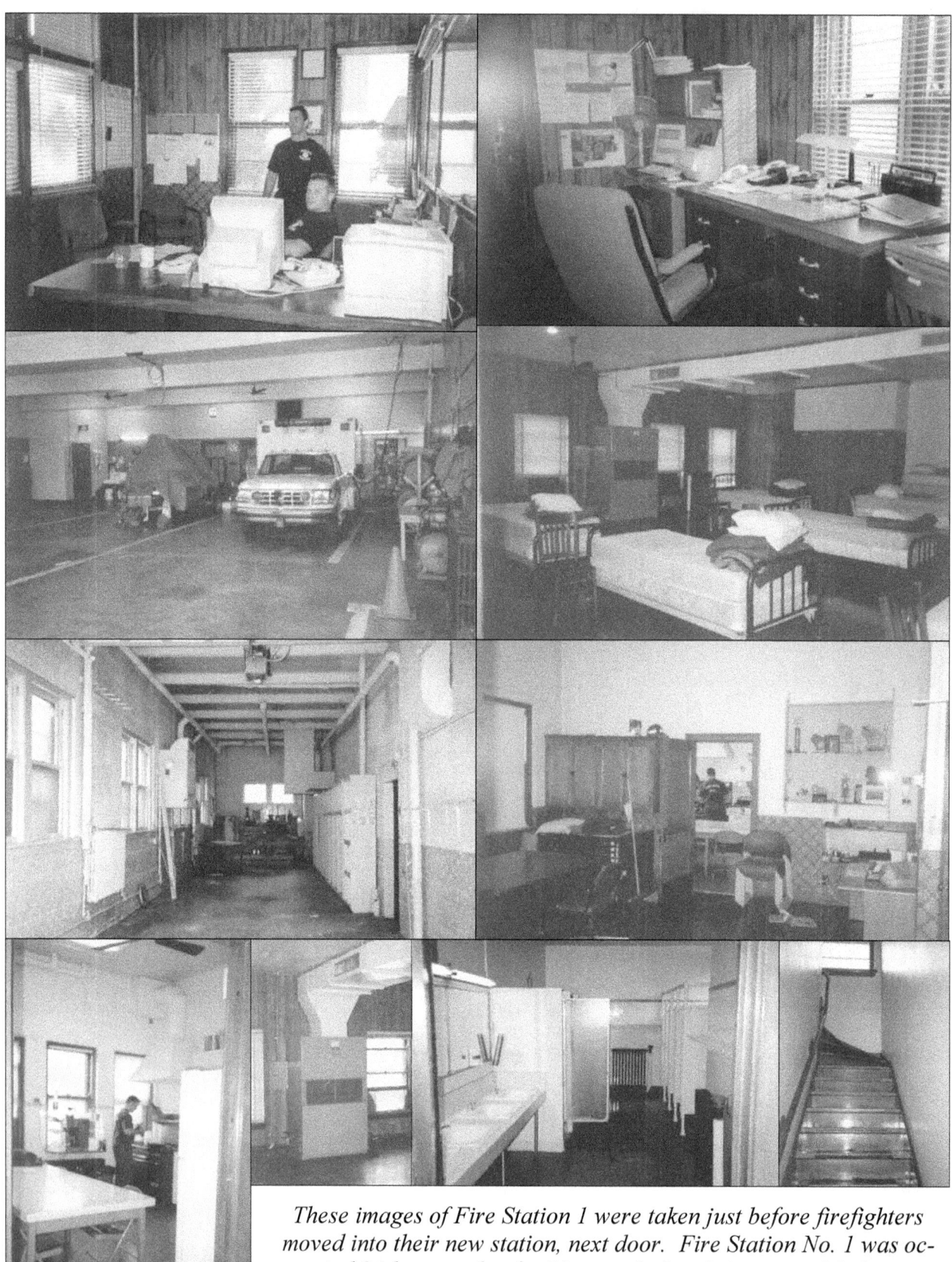

These images of Fire Station 1 were taken just before firefighters moved into their new station, next door. Fire Station No. 1 was occupied 24-hours a day for 73 years before being remodeled into a fire department administrative building in 2003.

Fire Administration Building
7332 W. National Avenue

Immediately after the last firefighter moved out of the old building, demolition crews moved in. Old Fire Station No. 1 was to become the new headquarters of the fire department. Plunkett Raysich Architects had been hard at work with fire administrators to design a building that would keep the attractive architectural design components of the original building, but also provide a new educational area and meeting space, record storage facilities, office space and computer server equipment. In the basement, a physi-

Immediately after firefighters moved into their new station, next door, Riley Construction began work on the renovation of the old firehouse into a Fire Administrative Building.

Spring, 2003

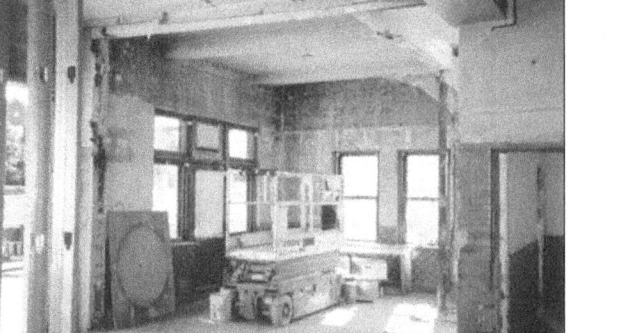

Riley Construction Company began remodeling Fire Station No. 1 in March of 2003. These photos show some of the work to the old apparatus floor that was being turned into a department training facility.

101

Station 1 and Police Department, February 7, 1993

Original Station 1 and new Station 1, May 12, 2003

Administrative Building and Station 1, June 1, 2004

cal fitness area was essential. And the entire building was to be handicapped-accessible and gender-neutral; neither of which had been a consideration for the 1929 fire station.

Riley Construction from Racine won the bid, and was hired as the general contractor for the project, as well as Fire Station 3's remodeling which was being performed simultaneously. The renovation was completed for $1.8 million, $100,000 less than the Common Council resolution for the project had allotted. It was completed in the spring of 2004.

Upon completion, all administrative offices, including training and fire prevention, moved to the newly-renovated office building. All administrative functions of the department could now be performed without interfering with or depending upon the fire suppression and emergency medical services staff. This separation improved the efficiency of all units, and provided much-needed storage and operational space for each.

Fire Station No. 2
2040 S. 67th Place

In the early 1950's the City was growing

rapidly to the south and west, and the need for additional fire protection became essential. This growth resulted from the annexation of at least six separate sections of land to the west and south. City administrators were interested in enhancing the ability of the City to serve residents and businesses, but were also concerned with autonomy. Mayor Klentz told the West Allis Star that without these annexations, the city would soon be "surrounded and choked" by Milwaukee.

As it grew, the city was divided into a north and south side by the Chicago and Northwestern Railroad tracks. Trains ran along the tracks every 15 to 30 minutes, 24-hours a day, and traversing the crossings was a difficult task for responding fire companies. The railroad served many industries to the north and along their route, but the densely populated south side was severely lacking in fire response times.

Chief Henry Nelson was able to convince the City that a fire station near the railroad underpass and trolley line of West Becher Street would serve the City well. On August 30, 1954 ground was broken for the City's Fire Station No. 2.

The new station was touted as one of the "...finest, most modern institutions anywhere." (WA Star, 8/22/1956). Station 2 was designed to include the department's maintenance garage, administrative offices, training facility and staffing for an engine and a ladder company, rescue squad and a battalion chief.

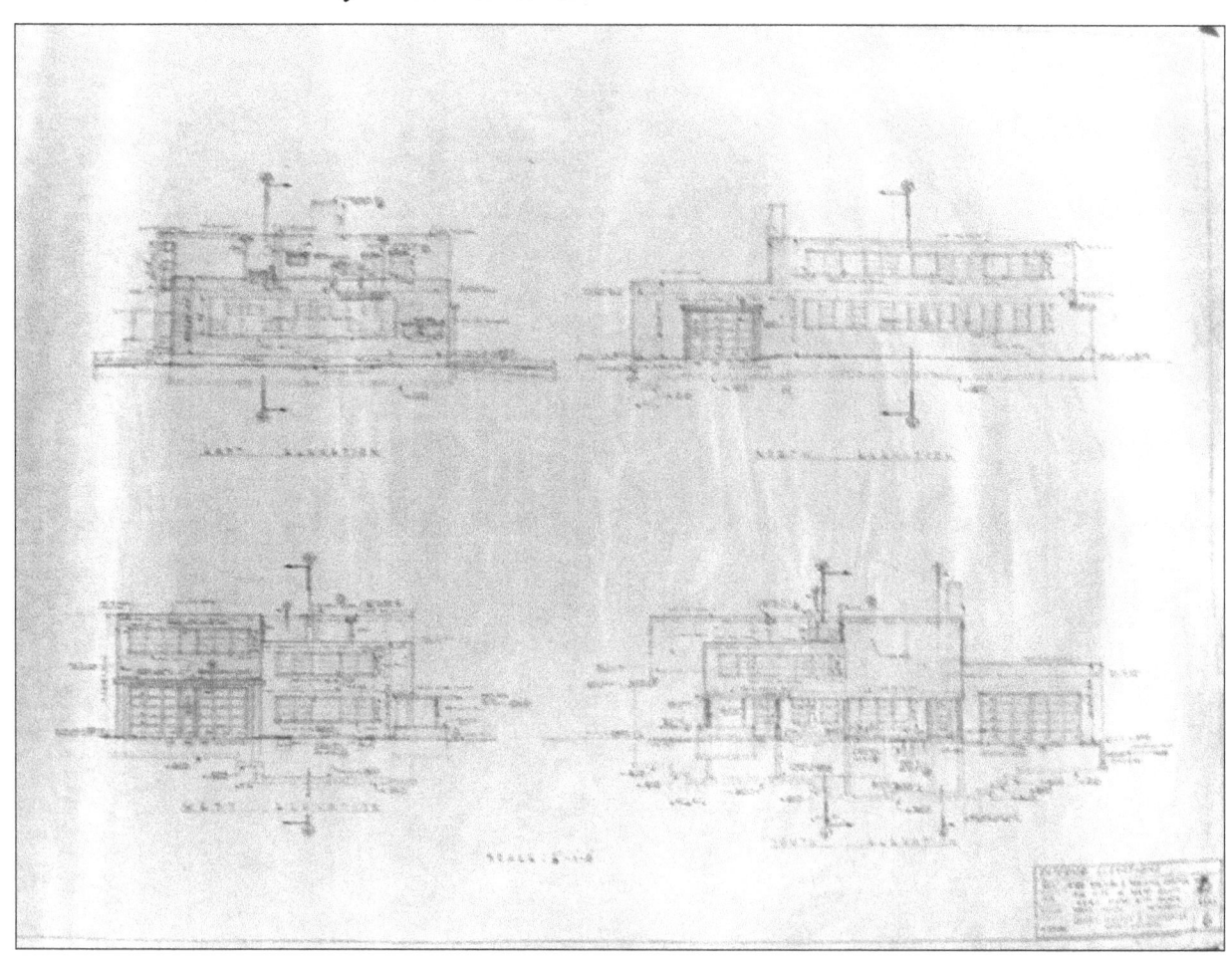

Blueprints used in the construction of Fire Station No. 2, 2040 S. 67th Place
Darby, Bogner & Assoc. Architects & Engineers, March 15, 1954

Open House Saturday At New Fire Station

Cornerstone Laying At Library Branch Set for Same Date

On Saturday, March 24, the residents of West Allis will have their first invitation to visit the new fire station located at 2040 S. 67th pl., on the corner of S. 67th and W. Becher sts. The event is scheduled to start at 2:30 p.m. and the new buildings will be open to the public until 5 p.m. in the afternoon, and then again from 7 p.m. to 10 p.m. in the evening.

According to Fire Chief Henry Nelson, invitations have been extended to the mayor of West Allis, the city council and other civic officials.

In conjunction with the open house program scheduled for the new fire house, Miss Margaret Paulus, chief librarian for the city of West Allis, announced that a cornerstone laying ceremony will be held at the new branch library directly adjacent to the fire house, starting at 2 p.m. on the same day, Saturday, March 24.

Costs $93,000

The new branch library will occupy 2700 square feet of space, and will cost approximately $93,000 when completed, including all of the furnishings and fixtures. It will provide much needed shelf space for the city's growing collection of books and other reading materials, and the completion date is scheduled for sometime in July, 1956.

The cornerstone for the new firehouse was dedicated on Sunday, December 19, 1954. It is one of the finest, most modern institutions to be found anywhere, and boasts of the latest in fire fighting equipment. In addition to the main building which houses personnel and the garage for the fire fighting apparatus, the new station has a completely modern training tower for the purpose of schooling its firefighters in the latest developments in the fighting of fires and rescue operations.

Construction was completed in October of 1955, and in December the fire department moved into the new building.

Public Invited

The public is cordially invited to attend the open house ceremonies on Saturday, and in order to assure all of the visitors a thorough tour of the main building and training center, Chief Nelson stated that all personnel on duty would serve as guides and answer any questions that the public might have to ask.

Above: Chief John Morch and Alarm Operator Les Barden in the new communications center at Fire Station No. 2

Left: The August 22, 1956 issue of the West Allis Star announces Fire Station 2's Open House.

Fire Station No. 2
2040 S. 67th Place
Darby, Bogner & Associates, Architects & Engineers
Completed October, 1955

Station 2's Next 50 Years

For the next fifty years, Fire Station No. 2 served all of it's intended purposes and more. Several additions and small alterations helped firefighters address a multitude of new challenges over the years.

Some of the modifications included:
1. converting the second-floor handball court into a permanent training room,
2. relocating a residential garage to a location adjacent to the building for storage,
3. adding a roof-ventilation simulator to the roof of the maintenance garage,
4. adding a telephone switching room to a section of the basement,
5. relocating storage lockers for personal protective equipment to make space for the addition of a washer and drier for PPE maintenance,
6. adding air pressure and electrical shorelines for all apparatus,
7. building an underground and above-ground training facility east of the training tower,
8. adding an EMS cleaning facility to the apparatus floor,
9. providing a passive air movement system to the apparatus floor to move exhaust fumes,
10. adding a Battalion Chief's office to the third floor,
11. removing two of the three fire poles from the third floor and one from the second floor,
12. installing computer cabling throughout the building,
13. adding an office to the training room for an EMS administrator,
14. converting dead space at the rear of the apparatus floor into parts storage for the maintenance shop,
15. subdividing the maintenance garage to make space for a fitness room, and
16. establishing space for a candidate physical ability test site on the drill field.

As time went by, the department began to provide more services and space became a premium. And as space became reallocated, the ability to renovate the building without major changes was becoming more difficult. Department administrators began planning for major renovations that would address even more challenges that were ahead.

Heating, ventilation and air-conditioning problems were growing. The roof leaked on a regular basis, with firefighters building temporary "interior gutters" to protect work areas and equipment, valuable apparatus was being stored outdoors in a harsh climate that was damaging hundreds of thousands of dollars-worth of equipment. Also, since the only female employees of the fire department were office workers, no gender-neutral accommodations were available in the firehouse, and the ability to diversify the workforce would be nearly impossible on a small scale.

Fire Station No. 2 Remodeling

In 2001, as a part of a department-wide fire station remodeling and renovation plan, Fire Station 2's building and service requirements could be addressed. In general, renovations addressed:

1. creating additional space for storage of equipment and apparatus,
2. installing modern heating and air conditioning equipment,
3. creating a gender-neutral firehouse,
4. utilization of maintenance-free materials to extend the useful life of the building, and
5. an attempt to predict and accommodate departmental needs for a fifty year time period.

Firefighters moved back into their remodeled station in January of 2006. As with the other stations, architects, contractors and ad-

Fire Station No. 2 served as the department's headquarters, training center and as a fire station for fifty years before being remodeled in 2005

These photos were taken just before the remodeling of Fire Station No. 2 in the early spring of 2005. Firefighters were moved into Stations 1 and 3 until the project could be finished.

ministrators were able to keep the project within its anticipated budget.

Photos on the next few pages show some of the various stages of the Fire Station No. 2 remodeling process.

Fire Station No. 3
10830 W. Lapham Street

While Fire Station No. 2 was being built to address fire safety needs on the City's eastern end, the rapidly-expanding western annexations needed attention. Although much less populated, these new sections held potential for significant grown.

Fire Chief Henry Nelson outlined a plan for City leaders that requested two stations west of 92nd Street. Although only one was built, the fire department's responsibility for providing protection required immediate action.

A temporary station was used while plans were made for a permanent location. The temporary station was a "Quonset-hut" type of facility with an unattached garage. It was located on the west side of State Highway 100, south of Greenfield Avenue. It was referred to as "Station 2" since it was actually occupied while the current Fire Station No. 2 was under construction.

When the actual western station was finished in 1956, it was located at 10830 W. Lapham Street and was officially named Fire Station No. 3. The station has served as the City's only fire facility west of S. 92nd Street for the last fifty years.

Station No. 3 Remodeling

As with the department's other facilities, an increase in services required a need for more storage space. Changes in the ways emergency medical services personnel discard disposable equipment and clean biohazards require cleaning areas that are separate from other cleaning areas. Passive exhaust removal systems were used in place of more effective systems that were available but costly. No accommodations were available for female firefighters.

As a result of a legal settlement with WE Energies, the City was able to address these deficiencies as part of a comprehensive fire station remodeling and renovation plan. The plan started in 2001 with the construction of a new Fire Station No. 1 followed by the renovation of the old fire station into a Fire Administration Building at 7332 W. National Avenue.

Fire Station No. 3 was renovation simultaneously with the Fire Administration Building. Riley Construction Company, a Racine-based firm, won the bid for the renovation of these buildings, using plans provided by Plunkett-Raysich Architects.

The Common Council approved a budget of $1,211,252 for Station 3's renovation, and the project was predicted to take approximately six months. Although contractors took an extra three months to finish, the budget was only $30,000 over estimate, and the department gained Council approval to continue the renovation project and look forward to Fire Station No. 2.

Alternative Fire Station

During renovation, the fire station could not be occupied, as planners had hoped. An alternative location was needed that would continue services to the City's western areas, keeping response times as low as possible.

Since the project was expected to last only six months, and was beginning in spring, an alternative location would probably not require a large, heated, weather-tight garage. And only six firefighters, four on an engine company and two on a fire rescue (basic life support) unit would be housed temporarily in the facility.

The West Allis/West Milwaukee et al School District had a building that seemed to be a perfect fit for an alternative fire station. The building was available from August through September of 2003, and a meeting between school and fire administrators gave positive results.

Parkway School, in the 2900 block of S.

The structure above was used as the second fire station for the City after the annexation of land in 1954. The photo below shows the "Quonset"-type houses that were used as temporary garages. The buildings were located on the east side of 108th Street, just south of Greenfield Avenue, and were used until a permanent station could be built. The apparatus assigned to the western part of the City were (from left, above) Engine 2 (1930 Pirsch 1000 GPM Pumper), Squad 2 (1954 Pontiac Station Wagon), and Tank Truck 1 (1954 Mack Tank Truck)

*Fire Station No. 3
Darby, Bogner and Associates
759 N. Milwaukee Street, Milwaukee, WI
Plans approved July 11, 1958*

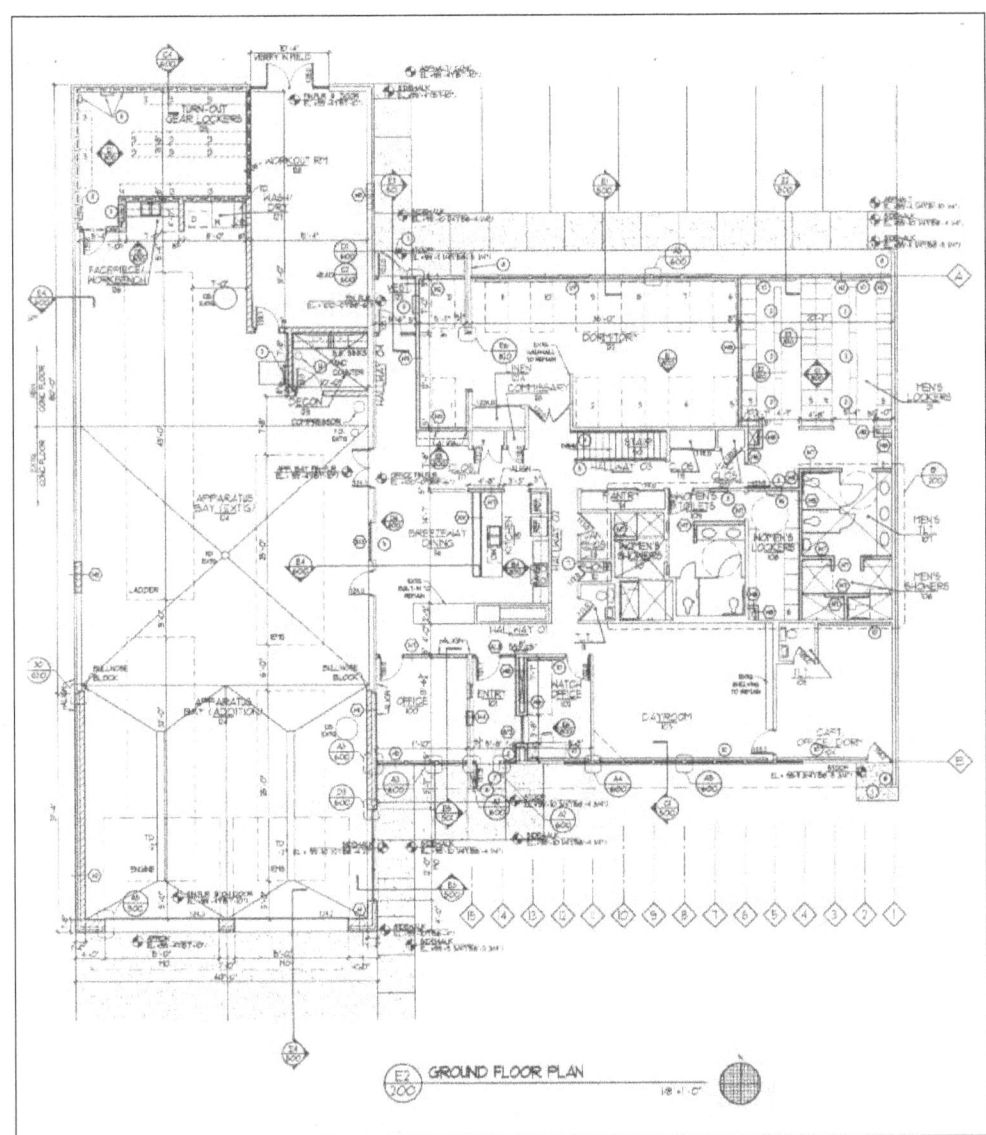

117

Fire Station 3's renovation project began in fall of 2003. Firefighters were temporarily quartered at Parkway School. The project was not finished until early 2004, so fire fighters spent most of the winter responding from their improvised fire station. Living space consisted of two classrooms with a vinyl tent for a garage. After moving into their remodeled quarters, the tent was loaned to Greenfield for their remodeling project.

The West Allis Star reported on the winter accommodations for members of Fire Station No. 3 at Parkway School while their building was being renovated. Bill Kurtz wrote the article with Mary Catanese-Pugens providing photos.

When completed, Fire Station No. 3's remodeling had addressed several of the buildings deficiencies. New, low maintenance flooring materials had been used, the garage was extended forward to provide more apparatus room, a new fitness area, a clean room for personal protective equipment, and an EMS cleaning area. The station had become gender-neutral, centralized heating and air conditioning units had been installed, all windows were replaced with energy-efficient systems and roofing materials had been replaced. After the firefighters moved in, a few modifications and adjustments were made to some systems, and the station should be ready to serve the community for the next 50 years.

Root River Parkway was selected. School Superintendent Kurt Wachholz was willing to allow firefighters to use the facility as part of a cooperative effort between the School District and the City to share services when it would benefit taxpayers.

Fifth-District Alderpersons Rosalie Reinke and Jim Sengstock were consulted to discuss concerns that neighbors may have when fire trucks and ambulances begin responding from their neighborhood. An informational campaign helped answer questions. In fact, neighborhood support for the effort was much greater than expected.

Project Delays Cause Weather Problems

Unfortunately, unexpected delays early in the project forced the occupancy of Parkway School to last into January of 2004. School administrators and alderpersons were very understanding of the delays, but the winter weather would not be so kind.

Early in the project, firefighters had erected a vinyl tent to cover the fire engine and protect their equipment from rain. As the weather turned colder, kerosene heaters were added and a watchman was required to monitor their effectiveness throughout the day and night. In addition, ceramic space heaters were placed in the engine and ambulance's passenger and patient compartments.

The consumption of kerosene and electricity, along with the additional months of driving over asphalt parking surfaces contributed to the small cost overruns of the remodeling project.

Finally in January of 1004, firefighter were able to return to their renovated quarters and resume service.

Finally Back in Quarters

When they returned, firefighters at Fire Station No. 3 found that the remodeling project had included:

1. new, low maintenance flooring materials had been used,
2. garage was extended forward to provide more apparatus room,
3. a new fitness area,
4. a clean room for personal protective equipment,
5. an EMS cleaning area,
6. the station had become gender-neutral,
7. centralized heating and air conditioning units had been installed,
8. all windows were replaced with energy-efficient systems and
9. roofing materials had been replaced.

The renovation project of Fire Station No. 3 met it's goals of providing a facility that would meet the department's needs for the next fifty years.

Chapter 4

Fire Apparatus

In 1905, the Village of West Allis purchased two hand-drawn hose carts, one of which is pictured at the right. They were suitable for carrying at least 450 feet of jacketed hose, one solid stream brass nozzle and chemical extinguisher. The cart had a T-shaped handle for two firefighters to drag it side-by-side, and a rope could be extended to the front to allow other firefighters to help move the cart, since all of the village's streets were dirt (or mud). A gong mounted inside the left wheel gave warning to pedestrians that firefighters were responding. One two-wheeled hose cart and equipment was kept at the barn of Frank Rock on 65th Avenue near Greenfield Ave. (present day S. 73rd St. & W. Greenfield Ave.) for $2.00 per month. The other was kept at the barn of M. Peters at the corner of 53rd Ave. and Greenfield Ave. (present day S. 62nd St & W. Greenfield Ave.). Mr. Peters agreed to store the fire equipment at no charge.

Above: The team of horses on the left is hitched to a combination hose and chemical wagon, with a 40-gallon chemical tank, two six-gallon hand fire extinguishers and 1000 feet of 2 ½" jacketed hose. The team on the right draws a ladder wagon carrying six 12-foot and six 16-foot ladders. The ladders were constructed such that each 12-foot section could be attached to each 16-foot section to form an extension ladder. Before moving into the station shown here in 1906, these rigs were kept at the livery barn of G. H. Jung (a local undertaker) on State Ave. (present day S. 81st Street) for $2.00 per month.

Upper left: The department's horse-drawn ladder truck prior to 1921, when a motorized Seagrave Service Truck replaced it. Here it appears to be part of a parade, possibly July 4th. Note the address on the building to the left (6209). This was the block between 62nd and 63rd Avenues on Greenfield Avenue. After the street renumbering in 1931, 62nd Avenue became S. 70th Street and 63rd Avenue became S. 71st Street. The brick building in the center still stands on the south side of the 7000 block of W. Greenfield Avenue.

Center left: West Allis' horse-drawn chemical wagon participates in the parade as well.

Right, Chief Peter Burbach is seated in the Chief's Buggy, sometime around 1906. Note the firefighter to his right pointing a 2 1/2" brass nozzle at the photographer.

122

Left, Chief Edwin Bryant is photographed with the department's first horse-drawn ladder truck. In 1946 the City was celebrating it's 40th anniversary, and the truck was prepared to participate in the parade. This is the same truck pictured 40 years earlier on the opposite page. It is now on exhibit in the Phoenix Fire Museum in Phoenix Arizona (below)

West Allis Volunteer Fire Department

PETER H. BURBACH, CHIEF
J. L. MERVILLE, SEC'Y

West Allis, Wis., June 28, 1916. 191__

TO THE BOARD OF POLICE AND FIRE COMMISSIONERS.

I hereby reccommend that the old hose and chemical wagon that is now at the ward shed at Mitchell Street, be motorized with a suitable chassis. I have been looking around at the different makes of chasis and find that the Nash Jeffrey Co. of Kenosha make about the most suitable. Their chasis are good and reasonable, with a good reputation from Fire Apparatus builders. Their one and half ton chasis sells at $1575. It would cost the city of West Allis practically $1800 to get another motor driven apparatus. This would be about one half the cost of a machine of the same type boughten new.

Respectively submitted,

Peter W. Burbach
CHIEF FIRE DEPT.
WEST ALLIS, WIS.

In his persistent attempts to motorize the department, Chief Burbach wrote this letter to the Board of Police and Fire Commissioners. The Commissioners responded by directing the Chief to prepare bids for a motorized pumper. Later the same year, a 1916 Seagrave pumper replaced the horse-drawn chemical wagon.

1916 Seagrave 750 GPM Pumper
Title No. 1064228, Motor No. 635, Series No. 14664
Cost: $9,000

The pumper show above was the department's first motorized apparatus. Chief Burbach is wearing the white helmet and coat, standing on the right running board. Note the dirt road that is the present S. 73rd Street. Tire chains were standard until many of the streets were paved in the 1920's. The station behind these firefighters was located on the site of the current West Allis Fire Station No. 1 at 7300 W. National Avenue.

Seagrave Service Truck
350 Gal. Pump
Title No. 1064229, Motor No. 1414, Series 28326
Cost $11,950

The fire department's first motorized ladder truck. Ladders were all wood truss or straight beam, and were very heavy. This is a copy of the manufacturer's photo. Designated "Ladder 1", it served as a front line vehicle from 1921 until 1944 when it was placed in reserve, utilized only for multiple alarms or training exercises. Interestingly, the truck's steering wheel was on the right. It was removed from service and sold in 1954.

Above Left: Howe Reo Combination Truck Chassis
Ford Engine No. A93694, Car No. 98296
Curtis Automobile Co., $6,726.83
In 1930, the truck was traded-in for a value of $2,000 as part of deal for two Pirsch Pumpers
Reo crew: Joe Gimler (seated), Frank Oppmann (driver), Robert Miller and Florian Luckow

Above Right: 1916 Seagrave Pumper
Pumper crew: Master Mechanic Charles Clunie (driver), John Petrie (seated), Captain Joseph Hayes, Herman Matz and Henry Nelson

Above Left: 1921 Seagrave Service Truck
Ladder Crew: Asst. Chief Edwin Bryant, Harry Leideritz, George Burbach, Elmer Schoen, Joe Charles (driver) and John Fagg (seated).

Above Right: 1928 Hudson Standard Sedan, placed into service 5/10/1928
Engine No. 524451, Serial No. 810792
Traded in 1/25/1938 (18,048 mi.)
Crew: Chief Peter Burbach and driver Charles Schulz

October, 1931
Above left: Truck 1 (1921 Seagrave Service Truck)
Above right: Engine 1 (1916 Seagrave Pumper) note the solid rubber tires

Chief's 1928 Hudson sedan as it appeared in a 1929 photo. Chief Peter Burbach is standing in front of the car in the double-breasted dress coat.

Above: 1916 Seagrave Pumper (Engine 1) undergoes a pump test measuring its capacity to maintain pressures and water flows for fire operations.

Below: Engine 1 in its quarters ready for duty. The photo shows the eastern inside wall of the apparatus floor at the present site of the Administration Building at 7332 W. National Avenue.

*1930 Pirsch 600 GPM Pumper as it appeared in a manufacturer's photo.
Peter Pirsch and Sons Co., Kenosha, WI
(Pirsch vehicles were all hand built to the specifications of each buyer)*

*This vehicle had a 600 gallon per minute positive displacement "gear" pump. It was one of two similar pumpers purchased from Pirsch in 1930. It was received on 8/1/1930, and was placed in service on 9/25/1930 as "Engine 3".
Title No. 1159607, Motor No. 467074, Series 20KU733
It listed for $7,500, but a trade in of the department's Reo dropped the price to $5,500.*

Pumping water on a cold day in January, 1937.

*1930 Pirsch 1000 GPM Pumper as it appeared around 1950.
This vehicle was another of the two purchased in 1930. It also had a positive displacement "gear" pump. The windshield was added in 1952 to help protect the driver from the elements. Received on 8/1/1930, it was placed in service 9/25/1930 as "Engine 4", but renamed Engine 2 in May of 1931, since the Reo had been removed from service.
Title No. 1159606, Motor No. 262951, Series 16RB732
Cost $10,950*

Engines 2 and 3, the department's 1930 Pirsch Pumpers, as they appeared in 1945 on the apparatus floor of the department's only fire station. It is the site of the present Administration Building (7332 W. National Avenue). The apparatus floor on which they are parked is now the department's training room.

Engine 3

1930 Pirsch 600-GPM Pumper

Below: The two 1930 pumpers on these pages as they appear today, owned privately and displayed for special events and shows.

Photo courtesy Jim Ley

Photo courtesy Jim Ley

Engine 2

*1930 Pirsch
1000 GPM
Pumper*

Left: The Chief's 1948 Pontiac and the Assistant Chief's 1954 Ford Customline as they appeared in 1954. The Customline was a 4-door, 8 cylinder vehicle purchased from Knipple Selig Co. and received on July 13, 1954.

1942 GMC Emergency Squad Truck
Model CCX-302, Title No. A7511643, Motor No. C23606293, Serial No. 22564
Cost $3,926.18

About the time World War II started, the department purchased its first rescue squad. It was a GMC commercial unit and was nicknamed "The Pie Wagon". It was a heavy-duty rescue unit carrying various tools, hydraulic jacks, heavy ropes, spotlights and first-aid kits. It also had an Emerson & Johnson Resuscitator (E&J). The E&J was used on unconscious persons to help restore breathing. With a tight-fitting face mask that sealed the mouth and nose within the mask, oxygen was forced into and withdrawn from the lungs in a normal breathing rate. It was also used on heart attack victims if there was no heartbeat.

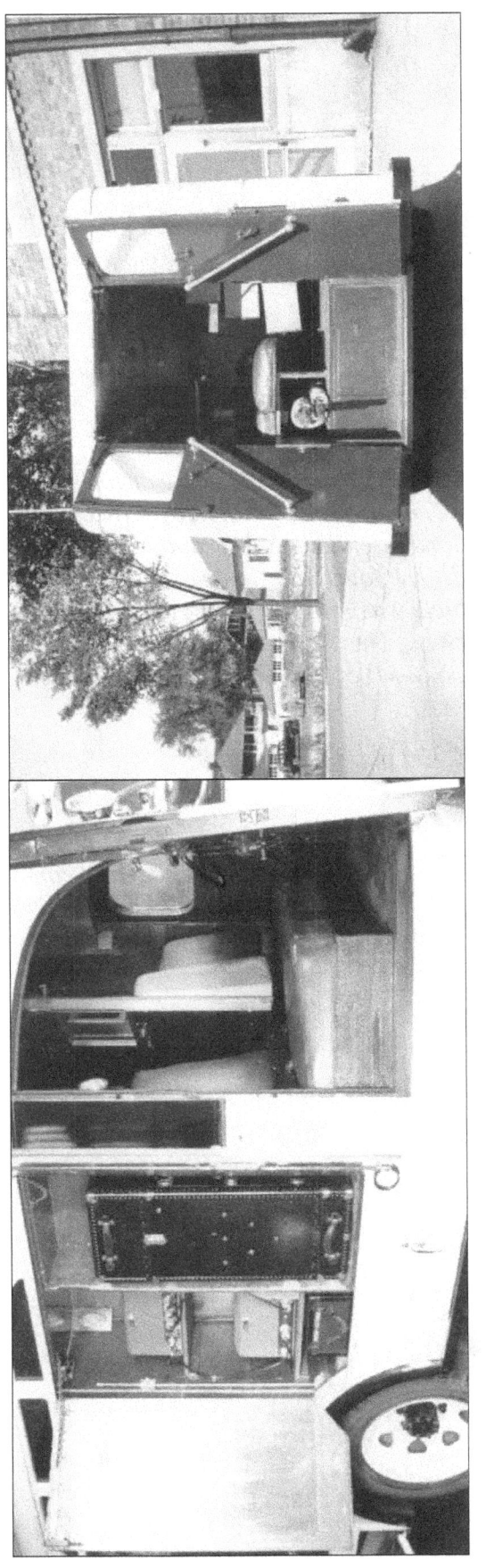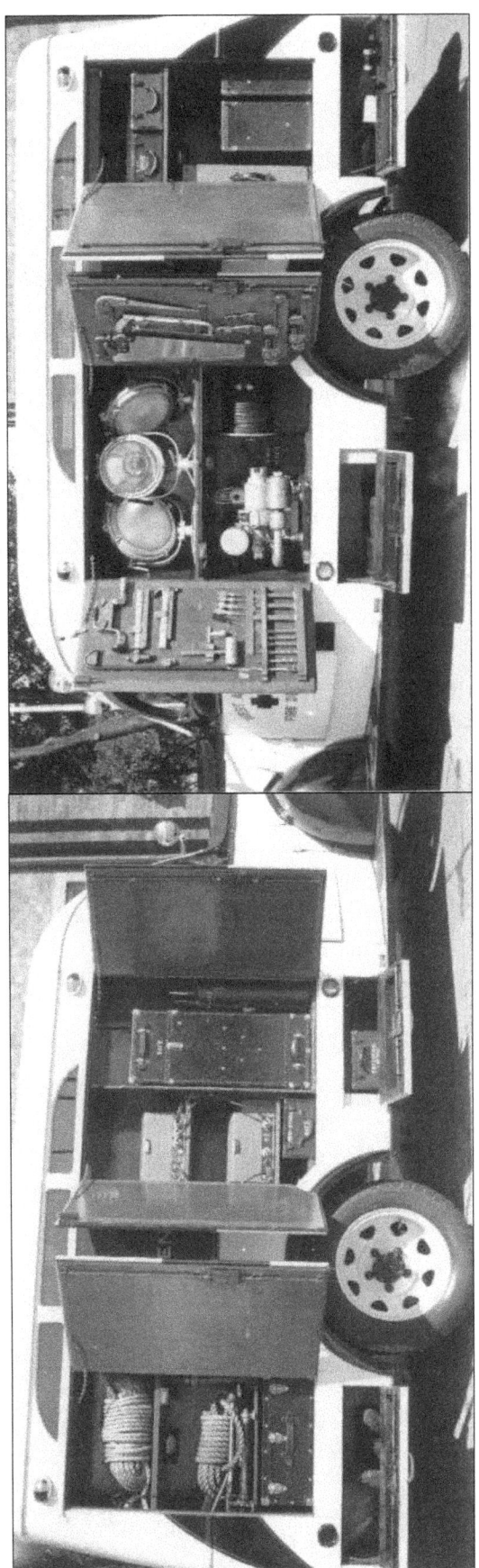

These photos show the equipment carried within the "Piewagon's" compartments. On the upper right, the stationary patient cot is visible with the back doors open. Stored under the cot is a rolled up canvas stretcher. Also visible are the many lights, extrication tools, ropes and small tools that added to the versatility of this unit.

133

Members of the Board of Police and Fire Commissioners pose in from of the department's new aerial ladder truck when it is placed into service in 1944. The ladder was lifted by a hydraulic ram and extended by cables. The three aluminum sections extended 65 feet, and a ten-foot fourth section could be installed and pushed up by hand. The fourth section was never used, and was stored in the basement at Station 1 until the vehicle was retired. The ground ladders were wood, straight beam and truss and were very heavy. The 50-foot extension ladder weighed over 200 lbs and required six men to raise it. Around 1955, lighter, aluminum ladders replaced the wooden ones.

1944 Pirsch 75-foot Aerial Ladder Truck, 100 gal. Booster tank
GK.145 Waukesha Motor, Serial No. 1349, 103.4 mi. on delivery, Motor No. 574196
Delivered 5/17/1944, Placed into service as Truck 2

Below, the very new and the very old. The newly received Pirsch Ladder Truck is seen in contrast with the department's original horse-drawn ladder truck. Forty years of technology separate the two. This was a publicity photo used to promote Pirsch Aerial Ladders.

Truck 2 undergoing maintenance service on the approach at Station 1 in 1950.

Truck 2 working at the Boston Store fire on Greenfield Avenue in December of 1953. Note the firefighters on the top section "locked-in" for stability, by placing their legs through the rungs. Modern aerial ladders are often longer and more powerful, and this practice has been replaced by using ladder belts to avoid injuries.

1947 Pirsch 1250 GPM Pumper, delivered 4/28/1947. Cost $13,000
Hale, Class B 2-stage centrifugal pump

This vehicle was assigned as Engine 1, replacing the department's first motorized apparatus, the 1916 Seagrave Pumper. On September 4, 1947 the West Allis Star explained that the new engine had been equipped with an automatic "Elston sander" for use on icy roads. It was also built with a compartment behind the driver's cab to provide protection for firefighters against the elements and inclement weather. These were the days of tailboard riding so this was a new (and seldom used) accessory.

1954 Mack Tank Truck
This vehicle was purchased because of the City's annexation of several surrounding parcels of land. It was placed into service on May 21, 1954. The truck was powered by a Mack Megadyne 122 hp engine. In 1968 an accessory Gorman-Rupp portable water pump was installed on the tailboard and the truck became a "Special Equipment Unit". The pump was placed at a static water source and used to fill the tank by drafting water. It could also pump pressurized water for fire fighting. The vehicle also carried a 1,000 gallon fold-a-tank.

Gene Frakes and Jim Baumann use the fold-a-tank and Gorman-Rupp pump at a rubbish fire near 99th and Burnham Street around 1968.

1954 Model F1000T FWD 1000 GPM Pumper, assigned as Engine 4
Manufactured at Four Wheel Drive Co., Clintonville, WI
Waukesha Motor Co. 240 hp engine, Waterous 2-stage centrifugal pump

1955 FWD 1000 GPM Pumper, assigned as Engine 5
Manufactured at Four Wheel Drive Co., Clintonville, WI
Waukesha Motor Co. 260 hp engine, Waterous 2-stage centrifugal pump

Station 1 apparatus as it appeared in 1954. From left, including the barely visible front of Engine 3 (1930 Pirsch 600 GPM Pumper), the Chief's 1948 Pontiac and the Assistant Chief's 1954 Ford Customline, Truck 2 (1944 Pirsch 75-foot Aerial Ladder Truck), Engine 4 (1954 FWD 1000 GPM Pumper), Engine 1 (1947 Pirsch 1250 GPM Pumper), Squad 1 (1942 GMC Emergency Squad)

1955 Pirsch 100-foot Aerial Ladder Tiller Truck, Assigned as Truck 1
Peter Pirsch and Sons Co., Kenosha, WI
Detroit Diesel 2-cycle engine, Hale centrifugal pump, 100 gallon booster tank
Replaced the 1921 Seagrave Service Truck.
Truck was returned to Pirsch 1/6/1976 for enclosed cab installation and new diesel engine, returned to service 5/5/1977.

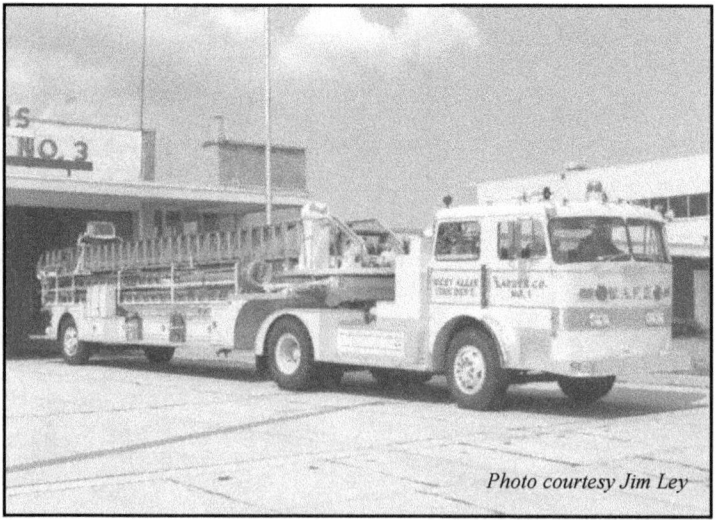

Photo courtesy Jim Ley

1961 FWD 1000 GPM Pumper
Waukesha Motor Company 265 hp engine, Waterous Class A 2-stage centrifugal pump,
500 gallon booster tank
Received from J. Bolan Truck & Equipment Co., Clintonville, Placed into service 11/6/1961

Below, firefighters training on Engine 6 in the summer of 1965 include (l to r) Stan Grabowski, Gerry Breznik, Truman Seltrecht, LT Tony Sparacino, Jim Hughes

Photo courtesy Jim Ley

Photo courtesy Jim Ley

1966 American LaFrance 90-foot Aero Chief Elevating Platform Truck. Delivered May 4, 1966

Although officially placed into service as Ladder 3, firefighters simply referred to this vehicle as "the snorkel". It was custom-designed by members of our department in cooperation with engineers from American LaFrance. The truck was very difficult to maneuver, especially around city street corners because of the length of boom that extended over the hood of the vehicle. In addition, ground ladder attachments on the sides of the truck, and above the compartments made them difficult to remove and replace. Although the aerial platform operation was very useful, these issues resulted the truck's early retirement.

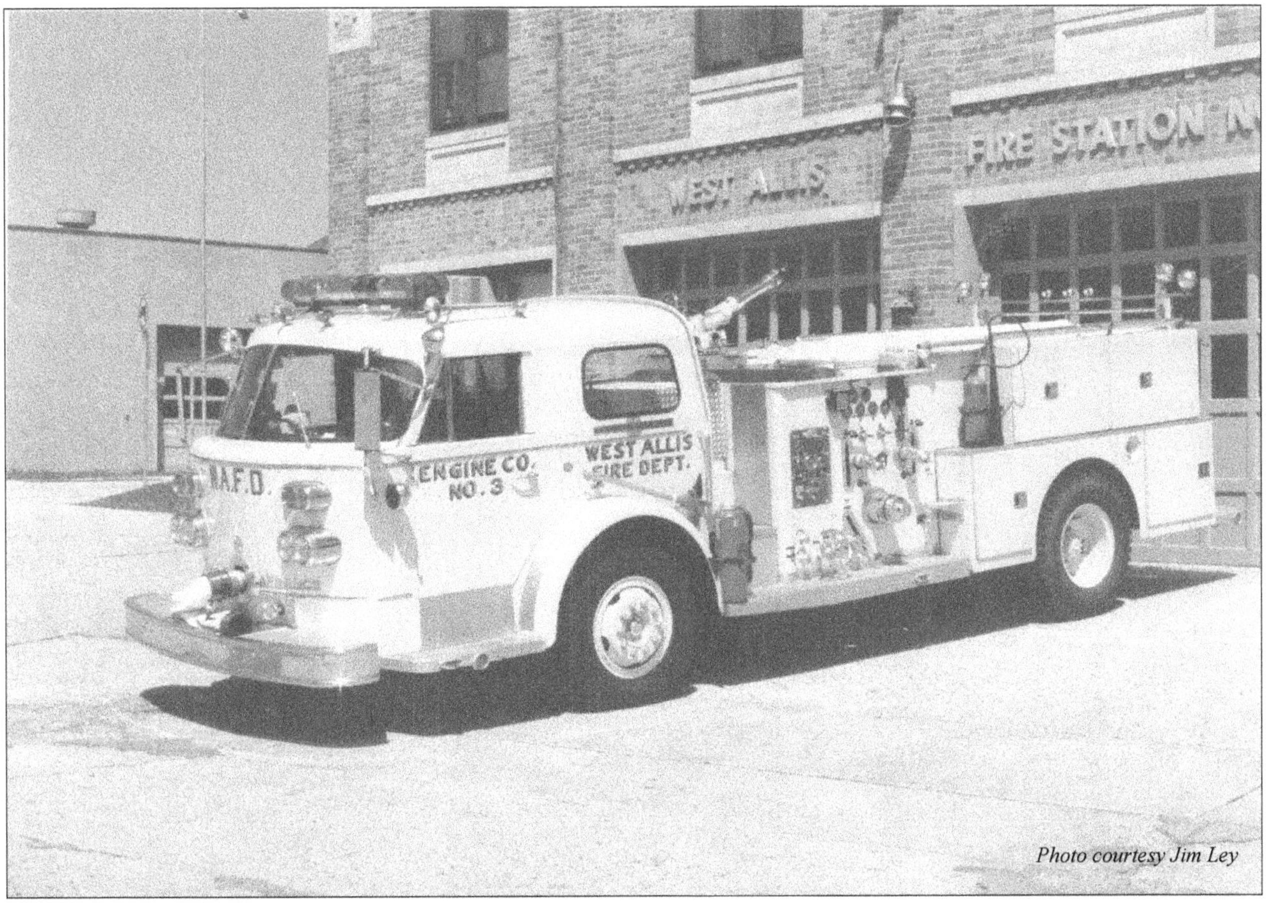

Photo courtesy Jim Ley

Fire Department's Newest Engine—Firemen run acceptance tests on the recently acquired fire engine ordered 14 months ago. The new engine replaces a 1947 pumper with a 1,250 gal. capacity; a 1930 pumper with 600 gal. capacity was traded in. The engine passed all its acceptance tests and has been in use for the past two weeks. Cost was $30,739. (Star Photos)

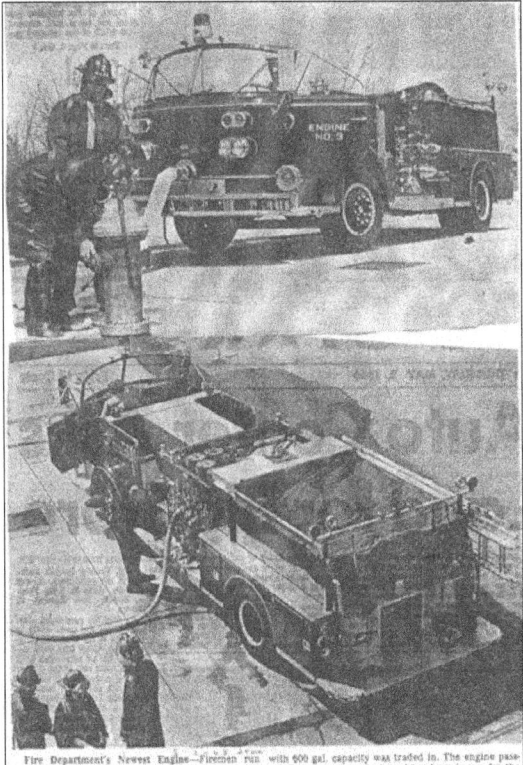

1968 American LaFrance 1250 GPM pumper
Continental Model L 290 hp engine
American LaFrance Class A 2-stage centrifugal pump
Cost $30,739

Replaced 1947 Pirsch 1250 GPM pumper and 1930 Pirsch 600 GPM pumper

The West Allis Star announced the department's new engine purchase on May 5, 1968 (left).

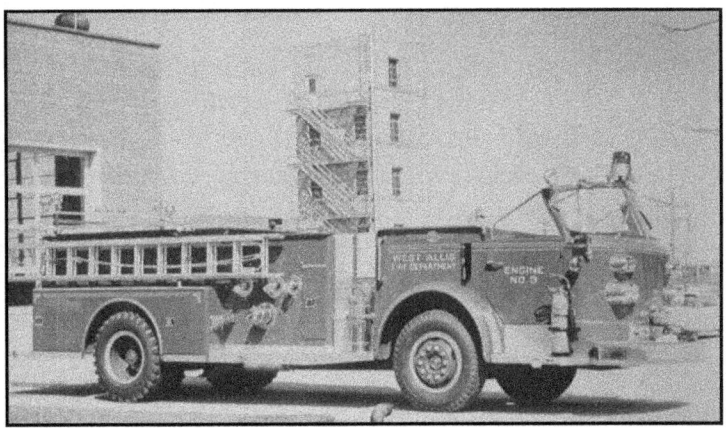

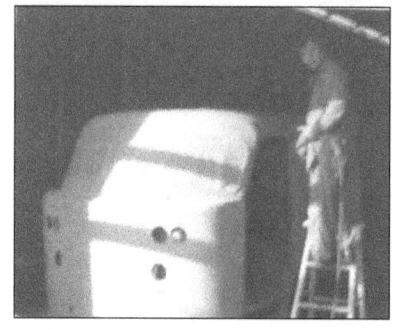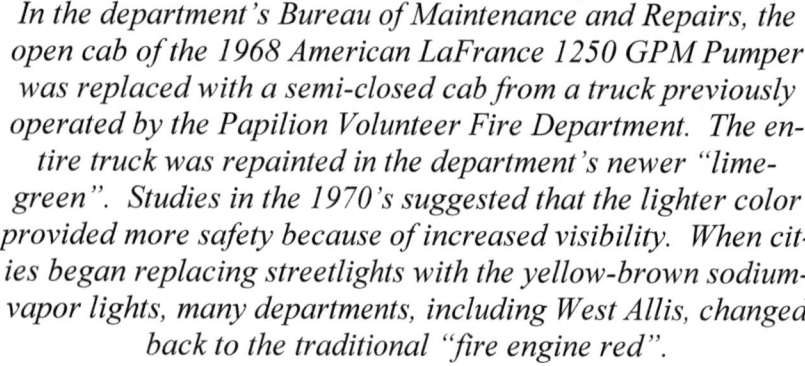

In the department's Bureau of Maintenance and Repairs, the open cab of the 1968 American LaFrance 1250 GPM Pumper was replaced with a semi-closed cab from a truck previously operated by the Papilion Volunteer Fire Department. The entire truck was repainted in the department's newer "lime-green". Studies in the 1970's suggested that the lighter color provided more safety because of increased visibility. When cities began replacing streetlights with the yellow-brown sodium-vapor lights, many departments, including West Allis, changed back to the traditional "fire engine red".

1973 Pirsch Pumper
4P1CA02DSLA000436 Cost: $78,000
Detroit Diesel 2-cycle engine, Hale Class A single-stage centrifugal pump, 300 gal. tank
Placed into service October 25, 1973, as Engine 4

1978 Pirsch Ladder 3203 $192,500
This truck was equiped with a 100-ft aluminum aerial ladder, 2500-watt remote-start generator, hurst jaws-of-life extrication equipment and complete NFPA ground ladder compliment. It was retired on September 26, 2003 and was sent to County auction (final odometer 54,111 mi., 3,371.5 hrs). The truck sold for $6,500.

Photo courtesy Jim Ley

1978 Special Equipment Unit (SEU)

The SEU came into service when the department downsized an engine company. The company was staffed by 1, 2 or 4 firefighters, depending upon daily staffing and responded to all fire alarms in the City. Two firefighters rode the tailboard, standing behind the collapsible windshield. The unit carried had a 250 gallon booster tank, a dry chemical extinguishing system and 5000-lb winch on the front bumper.

Milwaukee Journal

Photo courtesy Jim Ley

1980 Pierce Ford Pumper
Vehicle Identification Number: D80UVJJ7557,
Cost: $79,500

Photo courtesy Jim Ley

1986 3D Ford Pumper, 1FDYK90R8GVA11904, $136,500
Placed in service as Engine 3, moved to Engine 1 in 1994

1990 Pierce Javelin Pumper
Vehicle Identification Number: 4P1CAO2D2LA00436, Cost: $189,842

This was the department's first fire apparatus with an enclosed firefighter compartment, required by improved safety standards. The vehicle's 750-gallon booster tank stood vertically between the firefighters and the pump and pump panel. The Javelin's engine was located in the rear, beneath the hose load, creating the need for a special suspension system which received numerous maintenance adaptations over the first ten years of the vehicle's operation. The truck was purchased at a substantial savings because of the prototypical rear engine and because it had been used by Pierce as a demonstrator. This vehicle also began the department's return to red fire apparatus. Over the next 14 years, all apparatus were either refurbished and painted, or were purchased red.

Left: The old and the new. The Pierce Javelin is show with the 1954 FWD engine that was retired upon it's arrival.

Photo courtesy Jim Ley

*1991 Seagrave Ladder
1F9FW38J8MCST2053 $356,000*

In September of 2003, this truck was sent to the Pierce Manufacturing body plant in Weyauwega for body work and to be painted red. Ladder 2 was the last lime-green fire truck in West Allis.

Right: DPW maintenance supervisor Gordy Pabrocki (light blue shirt) inspects the body work and primer coat before the truck is painted.

1994 Pierce Dash 1250 GPM Pumper 4P1CT0254RA000486 $236,747

2004 Pierce Dash Ladder Truck, 4P1CT02W53A003259, $534,575, 105-foot steel aerial lad-

Engine 3 and Ladder 3 on a spring, 2005 morning, parked on W. National Avenue in front of the West Allis Public Library.

2005 Pierce Dash Engine
This 1250 gpm pumper was equipped with a compressed-air foam system that injects class-A foam into water used for firefighting. The foam reduces the water's surface tension and enhances it's penetration and coating ability. These features enable firefighters to use less water and reduce damage.

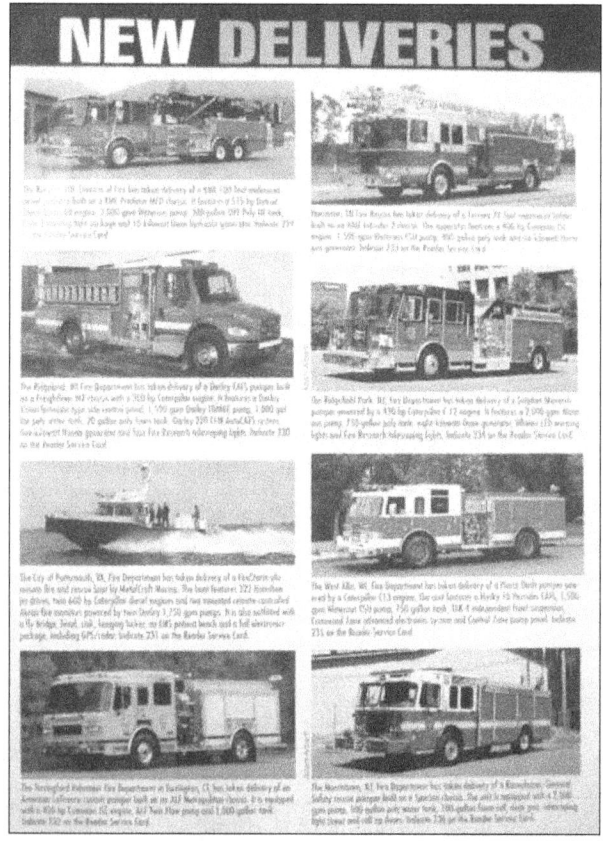

Above: In the final stages of production, department and sales reps examine the workmanship of Pierce Manufacturing employees.

Right: Fire House Magazine's "New Deliveries" section announces the department's receipt of the 2005 Engine (3rd row from top, right side).

Ambulances

West Allis firefighters have used a variety of ambulances to provide emergency medical care for residents and visitors. The following pages show examples of the types of vehicles.

Above: 1924 Nash, Operated by West Allis Police Officers who provided transport after firefighters provided first aid.

Left: 1942 GMC Emergency Squad Truck, Model CCX-302, Title No. A7511643, Motor No. C23606293, Serial No. 22564, Cost $3,926.18, retired 10/22/1957

Above: 1954 Pontiac Station Wagon, 8 cyl., Duckler Motors, received 7/30/1954, retired 4/10/1970 (28,751 mi.)

Above right: 1957 GMC Model 101 Rescue Squad, received from General Truck Sales and Service Co. on October 22, 1957. The new Squad No. 1 was placed in service 11/27/1957, retiring the 1942 GMC "Pie Wagon". Pictured with the new squad are (l to r) LT Art Siuda, Gene Frakes and Bruce Leifer.

1968 Dodge Van delivered by Doering Motor Co. (FR-3)

1970 Ford Van Model E200 Rescue Squad, FR-1 (received from Jack White Ford)

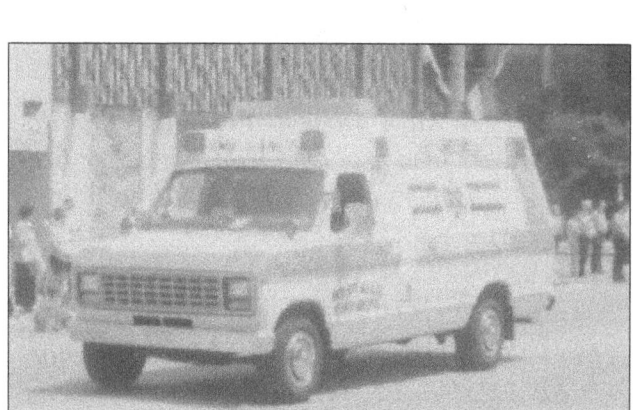

1979 Ford Type 1 Ambulance In service 11/30/1978 Fire Rescue No. 1

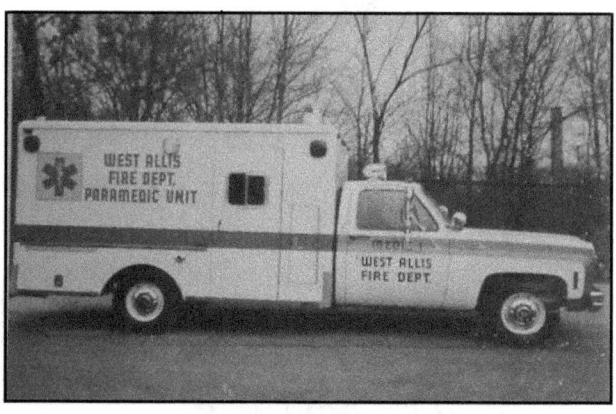

1973 Dodge Paramedic Unit (Medic 1), Rebuilt with new Pt Compartment and Chassis 12/1978

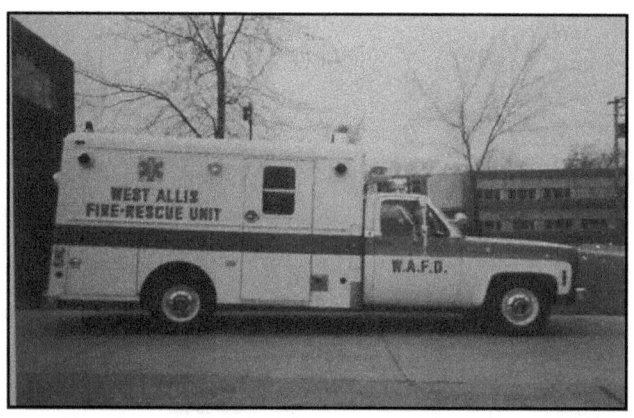

1974 Chevrolet Modular Ambulance "Champion Guardian", ID No. CCZ3341144589 (in service as Fire Rescue 4)

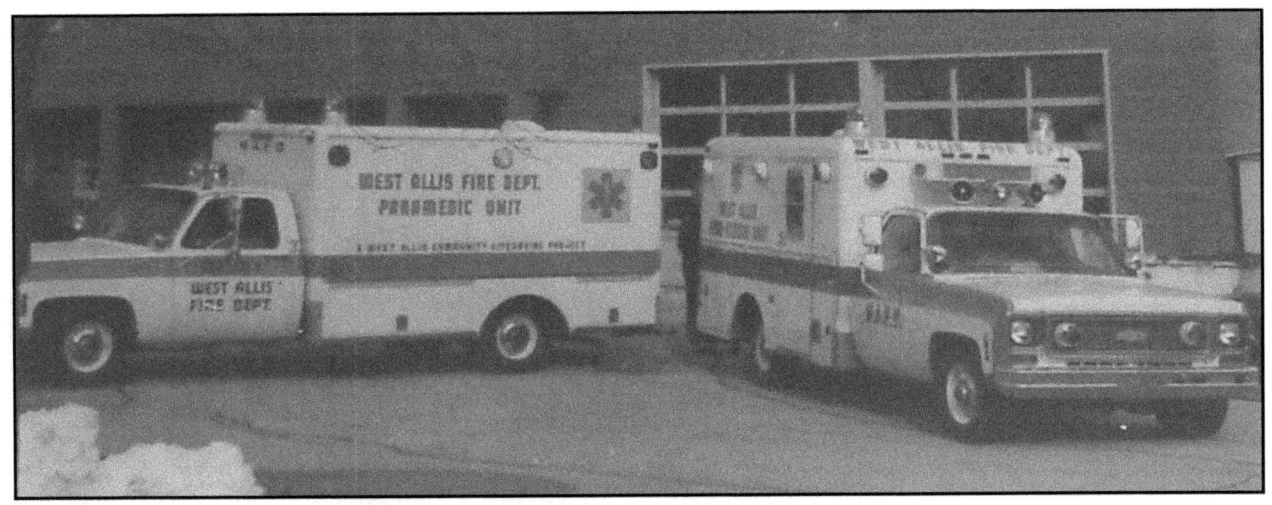

Milwaukee County's first Paramedic Unit, and it's backup

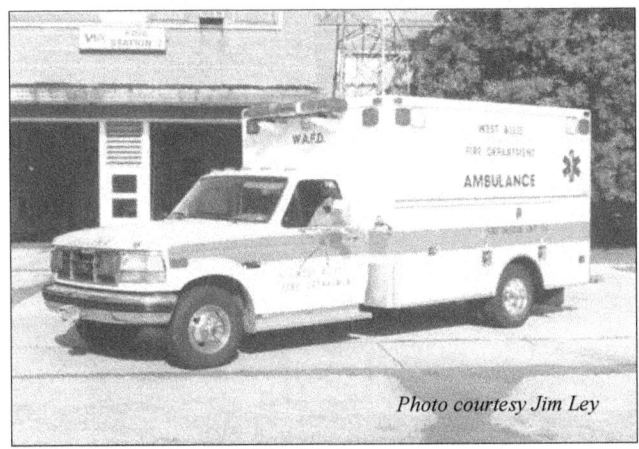

1993 Ford Light Duty Modular Ambulance (1FDKF37M8PNB09445) $30,760

1996 IHC Medium Duty Modular Ambulance (1HTSLAAM2VH411709) $91,568

2000 IHC Medium Duty Modular Ambulance (1HTMNAAM32H525118) $115,718

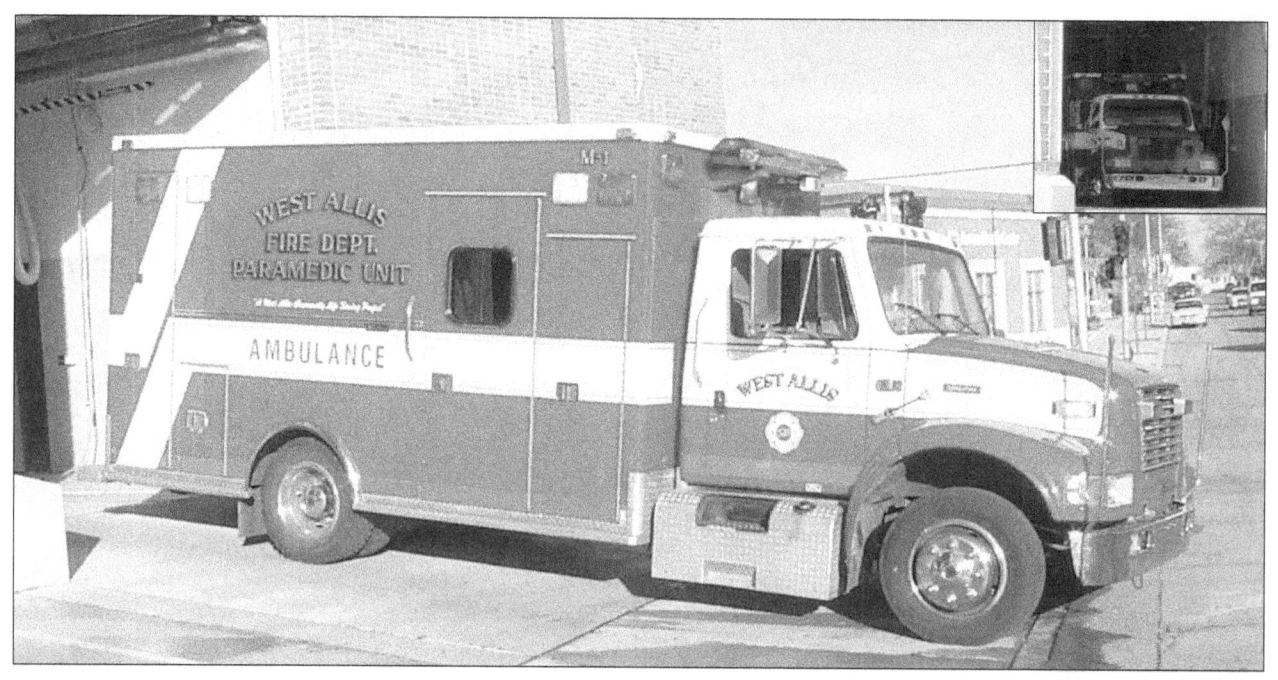

*2002 Medium-Duty International Harvester Corporation Ambulance
Med 1 cost $115,718*

*2005 Ford Light-Duty McCoy/Miller Ambulances
These twin units replaced both of the departments front-line Basic Life Support rescue units. They were slightly smaller than previous medium-duty units, but provided a smoother ride and could move through tighter places like the Milwaukee Mile's racetrack underpass. Fire Rescues 2 and 3 went into service in April 2005.*

Support Vehicles

A sampling of miscellaneous support vehicles, automobiles, utility vehicles and other apparatus owned and operated by the West Allis Fire Department

1978 Revcon
Purchased as an RV and converted into a Command Post by the Bureau of Maintenance and Repairs by WAFD personnel. The CP was retired in 2004 and replaced by the Milwaukee Metropolitan Sewerage District Tunnel Rescue Truck.
Right: The Command Post as it appeared when purchased for $5,000 in May of 1993.

1987 Chevrolet Suburban, VIN 1GNGR26K3HF158115, Cost $28,000

1997 Chevrolet 3500 Pickup 1GCHK34F8VZ140166 $27,866

Tunnel Rescue Vehicle
This vehicle was part of the equipment attached to the Milwaukee Metropolitan Sewerage District (MMSD) tunnel contract. The City of West Allis entered into the 5-year contract in 2004 to provide rescue for MMSD's tunnel contractors throughout Milwaukee County. The department's 50-person Technical Rescue Team received extensive training with tunnel contractors and performed numerous site visits over the course of the contract.

Haz Mat Trailer and Tow Vehicle
A 1985 International Harvester Corporation Chassis was equipped with cabinets, a 25,000 kW generator and various specialized equipment for use as a tow vehicle for the department's 1996 Haulmark Trailer. Members of the department's maintenance bureau installed a decontamination shower, detailed cabinetry and technical support equipment inside the trailer.

1998 John Deere Gator
Converted into a multi-purpose all-terrain rescue vehicle. The Gator can travel safely through crowds at the State Fair, travel through obstructions at the Milwaukee Mile, navigate areas around the County Park lagoons and rough terrain, and transport sick or injured persons on a stretcher with two rescue personnel on board. The vehicle has been copied by several local fire departments and similar design is in use at many stadiums around the country.

Photo courtesy Jim Ley

1985 IHC Support Vehicle
Vehicle Identification Number: 2HTNFTVR4GCB10152, Cost: $25,000

This vehicle was built by members of the department from an International Harvester chassis. The open firefighter seats and all compartments were built in the department's Maintenance Bureau. The rig carried a full ground ladder compliment and was used as a support vehicle and as a backup Ladder Truck on occasion. In 1996, the compartments were removed and fitted onto a new chassis with a 25,000 KW generator to be used as a tow vehicle for the hazardous materials response trailer.

History of Fire Department Apparatus

Year	Make	Model	Cost	
1916	Seagrave	750-gpm Pumper	$9,000.00	Retired
1921	Seagrave	Service Truck, 350 GPM Pump	$11,950.00	Retired
1924	Reo	Combination Truck	$6,726.83	Retired
1928	Hudson	Sedan		Retired
1930	Pirsch	600-gpm Pumper	$7,500.00	Retired
1930	Pirsch	1000-gpm Pumper	$10,950.00	Retired
1938	Packard	4-dr sedan	$1,388.00	Retired
1942	GMC	Emergency Squad	$3,926.18	Retired
1944	Pirsch	75-ft Aerial Ladder Truck		Retired
1948	Pontiac			Retired
1947	Pirsch	1250-gpm Pumper		Retired
1951	Dodge	1/2-ton Pickup		Retired
1954	FWD	1000-gpm Pumper		Retired
1954	Mack	Tank Truck	from WA Park Board	Retired
1954	Mack	Tank Truck		Retired
1954	Ford	4-dr Customline		Retired
1954	Pontiac	Station wagon		Retired
1955	FWD	1000-gpm Pumper	$22,650.00	Retired
1955	Jeep			Retired
1955	Pirsch	100-ft Aerial Ladder Truck	$64,400.00	Retired
1956	IHC	Civil Defense Rescue Unit		Retired
1956	Chevrolet	4-dr sedan		Retired
1957	GMC	Model 101 Rescue Squad		Retired
1958	Chevrolet	4-dr Del-Ray		Retired
1960	Plymouth	Station wagon		Retired
1961	FWD	1000-gpm Pumper	$29,860.00	Retired
1962	Plymouth	Station wagon		Retired
1963	Dodge	3/4-ton Pickup		Retired
1964	Plymouth	4-dr Savoy Station Wagon		Retired
1966	American La-France	90-ft Aero-Chief Elev. Platform		Retired
1966	Ford	Station wagon		Retired

History of Fire Department Apparatus

Year	Make	Model	Cost	
1968	Ford	Van Model E200 Ambulance		Retired
1968	American La-France	1250-gpm Pumper	$30,739.00	Retired
1968	Plymouth	Fury 4-dr sedan		Retired
1968	Dodge	Van Ambulance		Retired
1970	Ford	Van Model E200 Ambulance		Retired
1970	Ford	4-dr sedan		Retired
1973	Chevrolet	Bel-Aire 4-dr		Retired
1973	Pirsch	1000-gpm Pumper	$37,866.00	In Service
1973	Dodge	Van Ambulance		Retired
1974	Chevrolet	Modular Amb. Champion Guardian	$22,000.00	Retired
1976	Ford	3/4-ton F250 Pickup	$6,697.00	Retired
1969	International	Scout	from WAPD	Retired
1973	Ford	Automobile	from WAPD	Retired
1974	Ford	Custom	from WAPD	Retired
1978	Revcon	Command-post	$60,000.00	Retired
1978	Pirsch	Ladder	$108,000.00	Retired
1978	Chevrolet	Impala	$5,000.00	Retired
1978	Chevrolet	305 cu. In.		Retired
1979	Ford	Fire Rescue		Retired
1979	Pierce	Special Eq. Unit		Retired
1979	Chevrolet	Refurb Chassis & Box		Retired
	Jeep		from WAPD	Retired
1979	Chevrolet	Malibu Station Wagon	$5,028.00	Retired
1980	Chevrolet	Malibu 4-dr sedan	$6,750.00	Retired
1980	Pierce	Ford 1250-gpm Pumper	$65,202.00	In Service
1985	Ford	Tempo 4-dr sedan	$2,000.00	Retired
1985	IHC	Support Vehicle	$25,000.00	In Service
1986	Ford	F150 Pick-up	$6,500.00	In Service
1986	Ford	3D 1250-gpm Pumper	$136,500.00	In Service
1987	Chevrolet	Suburban	$28,000.00	In Service
1988	Chevrolet	Celebrity 4-dr sedan	$17,600.00	Retired

History of Fire Department Apparatus

Year	Make	Model	Cost	
1990	Chevrolet	Lumina 4-dr sedan	$21,000.00	Retired
1990	Pierce	Javelin 1250-gpm Pumper	$189,842.00	In Service as E2
1991	Chevrolet	Cavalier	$3,425.00	In Service
1991	SeaGrave	100-ft Aerial Ladder Truck	$356,000.00	In Service as L2
1992	Plymouth	Acclaim 4-dr sedan	$10,047.00	In Service
1992	Ford	Light-Duty Rescue	$30,391.00	Retired
1993	Ford	Light-Duty Rescue	$30,760.00	Retired
1994	Buick	Century 4-dr sedan	$13,929.00	In Service
1994	Chevrolet	Suburban	$56,173.00	In Service
1994	Pierce	Dash 1250-gpm Pumper	$236,747.00	In Service as E3
1994	IHC	Medium-Duty Rescue	$88,707.00	Retired
1996	Buick	Century 4-dr sedan	$15,042.00	In Service
1996	Haulmark	Trailer	$87,925.00	In Service
1996	IHC	Medium-Duty Rescue	$91,568.00	In Service
1997	Chevrolet	3500 Pick-up	$27,866.00	In Service
1997	IHC	Medium-Duty Rescue	$91,968.00	In Service
1998	GMC	Suburban	$36,230.00	In Service
1998	Chevrolet	Lumina 4-dr sedan	$16,504.00	In Service as C5
1998	Parker	Trailer	$906.00	In Service
1998	John Deere	Gator	$9,000.00	In Service
1998	IHC	Medium-Duty Rescue	$130,000.00	In Service as M1
2000	Chevrolet	Impala 4-dr sedan	$17,645.00	In Service as C2
2001	Chevrolet	Astro Van	$19,232.00	In Service as C7
2002	Chevrolet	Impala 4-dr sedan	$16,593.00	In Service as C4
2002	IHC	Medium-Duty Rescue	$115,718.00	In Service
2003	Chevrolet	Impala 4-dr sedan	$16,074.68	In Service as C2
2003	Pierce	Dash 105-ft Aerial Ladder Truck	$534,575.00	In Service as L3
2004	Chevrolet	Impala 4-dr sedan	$14,676.00	In Service as C1
2005	Pierce	Dash 1250-gpm Pumper	$323,993.00	In Service as E1
2005	Ford	Light-Duty Rescue (McCoy/Miller)	$99,422.00	In Service as R2
2005	Ford	Light-Duty Rescue (McCoy/Miller)	$99,422.00	In Service as R3
2005	Chevrolet	Suburban	$33,085.00	In Service as C3

Chapter 5

The Fire Chiefs

Fire Chief's Badge, 1906

Fire Chief's Badge, 2006

Eugene Braunschweiger

May 9, 1906 to February 14, 1907

Peter H. Burbach

February 14, 1907 to December 17, 1930

Edwin Bryant
December 26, 1930 to January 1, 1947

Henry C. Nelson
January 1, 1947 to June 16, 1963

John B. Morch
February 1, 1963 to February 2, 1978

Gerald Nolte
July 28, 1975 to July 25, 1977

Robert M. Block
February 2, 1978 to October 7, 1979

William J. Beres
April 10, 1980 to March 8, 1991

Raymond E. Schrader
March 4, 1991 to April 20, 1998

Steven J. Hook
April 20, 1998 to present

Chapter 6

Personnel

2006
Administrative Staff

Hook, Steven
Fire Chief

Dufek, Gregory
Battalion Chief, Operations

Huber, Mark
Battalion Chief, Operations

Piechura, Robert
Assistant Chief, Training

Mueller, Richard
Battalion Chief, Operations

Streicher, Gary
Assistant Chief, Operations

Bane, Steven
Assistant Chief, Em. Med. Services

King, Martin
Assistant Chief, Fire Prevention

Witt, Charlene
Principal Secretary

2006
West Allis Fire Department

Abbrederis, Randal S.

Bailey, Michael J.

Bandomir, David A.

Baumgardt, Scott J.

Becker, Daniel P.

Becker, Michael G.

Beres, Richard A.

Bloomer, Bradley A.

Boinski, Michael J.

Brehm, John M.

Breznik, Joseph G.

Brode, Kevin P.

Brown, Dale A.

Cavett, Jeffrey E.

Curtis, Brad A.

Danielsen, David

2006
West Allis Fire Department

deSnoo, Daniel J.

Dombrowski, Mark J.

Driscoll, Keith R.

Egeland, James P.

Enright, John W.

Faust, Michael E.

Fisher, Duane G.

Foley, Brandon J.

Freberg, Brad C.

Gale, Richard F.

Gapinski, Joseph

Gillard, Scott J.

Gorlewski, David S.

Grablewski, Michael J.

Gromowski, Scott W.

Gundersen, Michael J.

2006
West Allis Fire Department

Hauboldt, Jonathon R.

Hauenstein, Daniel T.

Heflin, Scott A.

Hubmann, Charles F.

Jansky, Joseph F.

Jarosch, David W.

Kaltenbrun, Steven J.

Kersten, Timothy H.

Kirchner, Daniel W.

Kjorlien, Jeffrey M.

Klaybor, Randal P.

Koenig, Benjamin J.

Koll, Brian E.

Koller, Craig A.

Kon, Steven M.

Kowalewski, Luke

2006
West Allis Fire Department

Krueger, Richard

Kurziak, Robert W.

LaDousa, Matthew S.

Langlitz, Bradley

Lazewski, Peter J.

Ledvorowski, Daniel S.

Lenske, Gregory D.

Levenhagen, Chris P.

Levenhagen, Daniel E.

Levenhagen, Joseph M.

Levenhagen Thomas P.

Liska, Scott

Machowski, Daniel R.

Madden, Michael D.

Maly, Curt

McCarthy, Emmet J.

2006
West Allis Fire Department

Meier, Joel A.

Muenchow, Thomas A.

Oleson, Todd A.

Paider, Guy J.

Palasz, Nicholas J.

Peterson, Steve

Pirlot, Keith J.

Pitman, Craig

Ponzi, James J.

Pooler, Mason

Portz, Scott W.

Potkay, Brian M.

Potochich, Bruce E.

Reinke, Christoph C.

Rohde, Peter D.

Scharfenberg, Japeth D.

2006
West Allis Fire Department

Schauz, Michael J.

Schilz, Richard S.

Schrieber, Brent W.

Shinkle Thomas M.

Snow, David J.

Snow, Jeffrey J.

Stanwood, Bruce G.

Staszak, Chad J.

Stenz, Richard J. Jr.

Stiglitz, Mallory

Strickler, Donald A.

Sura, Mark

Theim, Michael J.

Toepfer, Eric, J.

Tomczak, Mark J.

Volk, Dion D.

2006
West Allis Fire Department

Vorpagel, Timothy   Wendt, Mark R.   Werner, Russel A.   Wickerscheimer, Guy

Wiedel, Jeffrey J.   Zajdel, James M.   Zellmann, Kurt W.   Ziolecki, Chris R.

Members of the West Allis Fire Department Past and Present

Name	Rank	Start	End
Abrederis, Randal S.	Fire Fighter	2/22/1999	Present
Acker, James	Fire Fighter	4/26/1986	11/15/2004
Adams, David M.	Equipment Operator	8/16/1954	5/6/1969
Alfter, C.	Volunteer		
Allman, J.	Volunteer		
Ambroch, Ferdinand J.	Lieutenant	6/13/1959	6/30/1989
Anderson, Donald W.	Equipment Operator	3/15/1958	1/19/1987
Armstrong, Gordon	Fire Fighter	4/26/1954	4/22/1959
Baaske, Gordon L.	Battalion Chief	1/16/1949	2/18/1983
Bade, Marty D.	Civ. Alarm Operator	1/14/1974	12/18/1974
Baggs, Leonard	Fire Fighter	2/16/1947	2/25/1948
Bailey, Michael J.	Captain	2/15/1981	Present
Ballistreiri, Litterio	Equipment Operator	8/16/1953	3/23/1984
Bandomir, David A.	Fire Fighter	5/3/1999	Present
Bane, Steven D.	Assistant Chief	1/19/1985	Present
Baraga, Leonard J.	Lieutenant	10/10/1959	5/30/1989
Barbian, Norbert F.	Fire Fighter	8/13/1955	1/19/1983
Barczak, Russell J.	Captain	1/4/1969	6/30/1999
Barden, Leslie	Alarm Operator	4/15/1930	1/27/1967
Barnstable, Raymond L.	Equipment Operator	4/3/1965	9/13/1992
Barry, Ronald K.	Captain	1/9/1965	1/25/1992
Bartels, H.	Volunteer		
Bates, Ralph A.	Volunteer		
Baukus, Peter	Battalion Chief	1/1/1944	10/28/1977
Bauman, C.	Volunteer		
Bauman, James E.	Equipment Operator	9/10/1955	3/25/1987
Bauman, W.	Volunteer		
Baumgardt, Scott G.	Fire Fighter	1/25/1992	Present
Bayne, Bruce A.	Equipment Operator	1/8/1966	1/16/1995
Beatty, Michael T.	Fire Fighter	6/4/1988	11/27/1989
Beck, William	Fire Fighter	1/1/1927	7/2/1951
Becker, Clyde	Lieutenant	4/16/1948	10/14/1979
Becker, Daniel P.	Fire Fighter	8/2/2004	Present
Becker, Gilbert J.	Fire Fighter	5/19/1962	11/15/1987
Becker, Michael G	Lieutenant	6/21/1986	Present
Beekler, Lawrence	Fire Fighter	1/1/1944	8/3/1950
Benesch, Edward	Fire Fighter	7/10/1941	9/25/1947
Bennett, Frederick J.	Equipment Operator	8/7/1947	6/16/1985
Berens, John S.	Fire Fighter	4/26/1954	2/1/1984
Beres, Anthony	Volunteer		
Beres, P.	Volunteer		
Beres, Richard A.	Equipment Operator	7/16/1983	Present
Beres, William J.	Chief	2/6/1960	3/8/1991
Berghoefer, Richard M.	Battalion Chief	9/23/1972	4/16/2001
Berghoefer, Rodney K.	Equipment Operator	1/25/1964	7/26/1983
Berndsen, Peter A.	Lieutenant	8/3/1974	3/19/2005
Berninger, H. S.	Assistant Chief	5/15/1906	Present
Betzhold, Harry	Master Mechanic	5/15/1926	6/1/1948
Biedrzycki, Albert P.	Equipment Operator	8/13/1955	9/28/1979
Blankenheim, Mathias J.	Captain	1/16/1948	1/17/1987
Block, Neale R.	Equipment Operator	8/3/1974	6/17/2001
Block, Robert M.	Chief	10/16/1946	10/7/1979
Bloedorn, Arthur J.	Battalion Chief	5/24/1934	11/30/1969
Bloomer, Bradley A.	Fire Fighter	7/29/1989	Present
Boeder, Marvin E.	Equipment Operator	9/10/1955	1/17/1981
Boetcher, O.	Volunteer		
Boinski, Michael J.	Captain	4/7/1984	Present
Boiselle, L.	Volunteer		
Borelly, William	Alarm Operator	1/16/1949	02/29/73
Bove, Douglas	Fire Fighter	3/16/1953	12/8/1953
Boyle, Richard B.	Fire Fighter	8/13/1955	6/27/1959
Bradley, Allen J.	Equipment Operator	4/16/1954	1/17/1985

Members of the West Allis Fire Department Past and Present

Name	Rank	Start	End
Brah, Eugene	Fire Fighter	8/16/1954	4/12/1975
Brandt, J.	Volunteer	5/9/1906	2/14/1907
Braunschweiger, Eugene	Chief Engineer	8/13/1955	3/16/1984
Bregant, Joseph Jr.	Alarm Operator	3/30/1996	Present
Brehm, John M.	Fire Fighter	1/9/1965	9/16/1994
Breznik, Gerald J.	Battalion Chief	9/17/1994	Present
Breznik, Joseph G.	Equipment Operator	3/8/1975	6/27/2005
Breznik, Joseph Jr.	Battalion Chief	1/9/1965	3/15/1965
Breznik, Thomas E.	Fire Fighter	2/6/1960	6/24/1989
Brielmaier, Kenneth F.	Fire Fighter		
Brockhausen, H.	Volunteer	5/11/1998	Present
Brode, Kevin P.	Fire Fighter	2/14/1987	Present
Brown, Dale A.	Equipment Operator	5/15/1926	3/16/1940
Brown, Franklin	Fire Fighter	2/1/1930	3/11/1930
Brown, Peter L.	Fire Fighter	8/9/1937	7/5/1964
Brown, Richard	Equipment Operator		
Brunker, E.	Volunteer		
Brunner, G.	Volunteer	5/15/1906	1/1/1947
Bryant, Edwin	Chief	3/5/1931	1/16/1937
Burbach, Ernest	Fire Fighter	5/12/1909	7/15/1943
Burbach, George	Fire Fighter	5/15/1906	12/17/1930
Burbach, Peter H.	Chief	1/16/1949	12/31/1976
Burke, Bernard	Captain	8/9/1937	3/21/1966
Burns, Michael	Alarm Operator	4/15/1967	1/16/1998
Burt, Robert	Captain	2/6/1960	3/17/1986
Burtch, Walter J.	Captain	5/22/1952	6/5/1982
Candek, Erwin J.	Captain	6/17/1963	1/18/1982
Candek, Jean	Secretary	1/21/1989	6/1/2000
Cashmore, David B.	Equipment Operator	5/11/1998	Present
Cavett, Jeffrey E.	Fire Fighter	4/3/1976	3/2/2005
Cerull, Richard C.	Captain		
Charles, Joseph	Fire Fighter	5/14/1919	3/10/1943
Charles, Laverne	Battalion Chief	8/13/1941	5/20/1976
Chatham, James	Fire Fighter	4/20/1963	7/19/1965
Cheplak, Joseph	Fire Fighter	1/1/1944	2/6/1950
Clunie, Charles	Master Mechanic	11/12/1913	5/16/1934
Conway, W.	Volunteer		
Cortsen, Clyde	Fire Fighter	3/5/1931	7/7/1953
Craig, James R.	Battalion Chief	8/16/1954	3/17/1987
Csavoj, Anthony	Fire Fighter	4/26/1986	7/4/1993
Curtis, Brad A.	Fire Fighter	4/17/1993	Present
Dahms, John G.	Fire Fighter	1/23/1982	5/16/1988
Danielsen, David	Fire Fighter	4/14/1987	Present
Davis, Clark E.	Fire Fighter	9/10/1955	5/1/1958
Davis, D.	Volunteer		
Deakin, Kenneth E.	Captain	9/10/1955	4/20/1986
Deakin, Russell R.	Lieutenant	8/21/1961	1/17/1989
Debattista, Donald J.	Fire Fighter	8/13/1955	12/15/1967
deSnoo, Daniel J.	Fire Fighter	6/25/2001	Present
Dingel, William G.	Fire Fighter	4/26/1954	4/15/1959
Dobernig, Edward C.	Battalion Chief	3/15/1958	2/3/1990
Dobernig, Edward L.	Battalion Chief	1/17/1981	8/1/2001
Dobernig, Thomas D.	Captain	1/14/1984	9/29/2003
Dolan, Steven R.	Fire Fighter	3/29/1980	5/1/2004
Dolensek, Oscar	Battalion Chief	12/20/1947	2/3/1979
Dombrowski, Mark J.	Fire Fighter	5/11/1991	Present
Donnelly, Charles	Lieutenant	5/15/1906	
Doyle, Robert	Fire Fighter	1/16/1949	5/20/1959
Driscoll, Keith R.	Fire Fighter	4/12/1984	Present
Driscoll, Michael T.	Fire Fighter	9/17/1975	7/29/2000
Duchow, Donald C.	Captain	4/26/1954	1/20/1986
Dufek, Gregory J.	Battalion Chief	1/19/1980	Present

Members of the West Allis Fire Department Past and Present

Name	Rank	Start	End
Egeland, James P.	Captain	8/13/1983	Present
Eiche, Charles	Captain	5/15/1906	-
Eiche, J.	Volunteer		
Elertson, David T.	Equipment Operator	12/28/1966	3/16/1996
Enright, John W.	Equipment Operator	1/23/1982	Present
Evans, Richard	Lieutenant	3/16/1953	6/26/1967
Fabina, Stephen N.	Fire Fighter	9/10/1955	2/24/1985
Fagg, John	Captain	6/19/1923	8/31/1957
Farrar, Jack J.	Fire Fighter	1/6/1968	6/28/1998
Faust, Michael E.	Fire Fighter	10/24/1992	Present
Fischer, Russell T.	Captain	9/6/1935	9/12/1958
Fisher, Duane G.	Fire Fighter	3/30/1996	Present
Frakes, Eugene H.	Equipment Operator	5/16/1953	1/19/1986
Foley, Brandon J.	Fire Fighter	8/1/2005	Present
Franson, Bernard (Ben)	Volunteer		
Franson, Charles	Fire Fighter	3/5/1931	5/6/1932
Franson, Fred	Volunteer		
Freberg, Brad C.	Equipment Operator	1/19/1980	Present
Frievalt, Kieth N.	Fire Fighter	7/22/1967	2/1/1973
Galbraith, Robert	Fire Inspector	3/16/1953	12/6/1977
Gale, Richard F.	Lieutenant	3/21/1981	Present
Gapinski, Joseph	Fire Fighter	3/13/2000	Present
Gavigan, William C.	Fire Fighter	4/26/1954	1/17/1987
Gevart, A.	Volunteer		
Gevart, H.	Volunteer		
Gillard, Scott J.	Equipment Operator	7/7/1990	Present
Gimler, Joseph	Fire Fighter	7/8/1914	4/24/1946
Gleason, Gordon W.	Battalion Chief	2/6/1960	6/28/1989
Glittenberg, Fred	Volunteer		
Goelz, Donald E.	Fire Fighter	12/16/1980	12/17/2003
Gohres, John	Lieutenant	5/15/1906	-
Gorlewski, David S.	Fire Fighter	6/21/1986	Present
Grablewski, Michael J.	Fire Fighter	1/25/1992	Present
Grabowski, Stanley E.	Captain	2/16/1951	1/18/1985
Griglak, Michael W.	Fire Fighter	8/3/1998	8/15/1998
Groh, Marc R.	Lieutenant	10/1/1966	1/18/1995
Gromowski, Scott W.	Fire Fighter	8/2/2004	Present
Gudynowski, Gerald J.	Lieutenant	7/22/1967	1/1/1999
Gudynowski, John C.	Fire Fighter	3/10/1973	8/18/2002
Gundersen, Miachael J.	Fire Fighter	7/29/1989	Present
Haessly, James M.	Lieutenant	4/15/1967	1/20/1998
Haig, J.	Volunteer		
Hall, Terry	Fire Fighter	4/15/1967	10/14/1967
Hauboldt, Jonathon R.	Fire Fighter	4/19/1997	Present
Haunstein, Daniel T.	Fire Fighter	8/3/1998	Present
Hayes, Joseph	Assistant Chief	11/8/1911	8/1/1936
Hayes, William	First Assistant Chief	5/24/1934	7/31/1952
Heflin, Scott A.	Fire Fighter	5/11/1991	Present
Heid, E.	Volunteer		
Heid, Kenneth J.	Fire Fighter	1/25/1964	6/30/1989
Hendricks, Thomas E.	Fire Fighter	1/11/1969	2/11/1996
Herrmann, Eugene	Equipment Operator	1/16/1949	1/19/1980
Hinrichs, George H.	Battalion Chief	1/1/1944	3/26/1975
Hinterberg, Arthur P.	Civ. Alarm Operator	2/5/1975	-
Hoerres, Kenneth J.	Equipment Operator	4/26/1954	1/2/1985
Hokenson, John A.	Volunteer		
Holada, Joseph L.	Lieutenant	11/16/1947	3/31/1984
Hook, Steven J.	Chief	1/17/1981	Present
Horwath, Joseph J.	Captain	4/3/1965	1/17/1995
Howard, H.	Volunteer		
Huber, Mark A.	Battalion Chief	2/29/1980	Present
Hubmann, Charles F.	Fire Fighter	7/16/1983	Present

179

Members of the West Allis Fire Department Past and Present

Name	Rank	Start	End	Name	Rank	Start	End
Hughes, Hugh J.	Equipment Operator	2/6/1960	6/26/1989	Kirschnik, Harvey	Fire Fighter	1/16/1955	8/22/1977
Hunsicker, Alfred	Fire Fighter	2/1/1929	9/26/1959	Kirsop, Richard A.	Fire Fighter	9/10/1955	1/31/1985
Hutto, Clarence J.	Battalion Chief	4/15/1967	3/18/1998	Kjorlien, Jeffrey M.	Equipment Operator	1/9/1988	Present
Hutto, Eugene C.	Equipment Operator	8/13/1955	4/30/1988	Klaybor, Randal P.	Lieutenant	1/15/1983	Present
Jacobi, F.	Volunteer			Kling, Ronald M.	Lieutenant	10/6/1979	1/2/2005
Jagmin, Donald C.	Fire Fighter	6/6/1959	9/30/1967	Klug, Robert L.	Equipment Operator	4/26/1954	5/9/1983
Jameson, F.	Volunteer			Koehn, William	Volunteer		
Jansky, Joseph F.	Fire Fighter	6/13/1981	Present	Koehn, William	Equipment Operator	2/13/1942	2/7/1969
Jarosch, David W.	Lieutenant	1/9/1988	Present	Koelsch, F.	Volunteer		
Jastroch, Joseph	Equipment Operator	5/16/1952	10/1/1977	Koenig, Benjamin J.	Equipment Operator	3/3/1990	Present
Johnsen, Gary W.	Fire Fighter	10/1/1966	9/5/1972	Kolander, John	Captain	12/16/1948	1/6/1980
Johnson, Arthur	Captain	5/15/1906		Kolb, August	Fire Fighter	1/16/1949	9/28/1951
Johnson, Douglas R.	Fire Fighter	1/17/1981	2/10/1996	Kolberg, Merlin	Lieutenant	3/16/1953	1/27/1980
Jungbauer, Thomas M.	Captain	6/17/1976	8/1/2004	Koll, Brian E.	Fire Fighter	5/1/2005	Present
Kajtna, Elaine C. (Jonides)	Clerk-Stenographer	6/23/1952	5/16/1954	Koller, Craig A.	Fire Fighter	4/19/1997	Present
Kalamarz, Julius F.	Fire Fighter	9/10/1955	1/17/1988	Kon, Steven M.	Fire Fighter	2/22/1999	Present
Kaltenbrun, Steven J.	Fire Fighter	8/1/2005	Present	Kopac, Wayne D.	Fire Fighter	7/11/1959	7/23/1974
Kapitan, Frank S.	Equipment Operator	3/6/1952	3/21/1982	Koparian, Elliah	Fire Fighter	2/16/1954	8/31/1954
Kehlenbrink, John H.	Lieutenant	1/16/1949	3/31/1980	Koper, Albert J.	Fire Fighter	3/9/1991	4/1/1991
Kempf, Theodore R.	Fire Fighter	8/8/1964	8/17/1964	Kowalewski, Luke	Fire Fighter	3/13/2000	Present
Kerr, John T.	Fire Fighter	7/13/1968	6/17/1999	Kozlik, Jerrold J.	Fire Fighter	9/18/1965	8/1/1983
Kersten, Timothy H.	Fire Fighter	7/10/2000	Present	Krahn, John	Volunteer		
Kestelik, Robert J.	Lieutenant	9/10/1955	1/16/1989	Krueger, Richard	Equipment Operator	6/4/1988	Present
Kezman, Stephen C.	Equipment Operator	6/29/1959	12/17/1976	Kumershek, Robert	Lieutenant	1/16/1954	1/29/1980
Kiel, James M.	Lieutenant	10/29/1977	6/17/2003	Kurziak, Robert W.	Equipment Operator	3/24/1989	Present
Kimpel, Duane R.	Equipment Operator	3/24/1962	1/30/1988	Kuse, Harry	Assistant Chief	2/1/1929	7/6/1951
King, Martin M.	Assistant Chief	2/14/1987	Present	LaDousa, Matthew S.	Fire Fighter	8/1/2005	Present
Kirchhoff, Gilbert A.	Battalion Chief	10/16/1946	7/7/1974	Landry, Joseph J Jr.	Fire Fighter	7/16/1955	2/28/1985
Kirchner, Daniel W.	Equipment Operator	1/21/1989	Present	Lange, Gordon R.	Equipment Operator	7/16/1951	1/30/1984
Kirchner, Donald E.	Equipment Operator	3/16/1953	3/13/1986	Langlitz, Bradley	Fire Fighter	6/4/1988	Present
Kirchner, Vernon H.	Equipment Operator	1/16/1954	1/18/1985	Lau, David A.	Lieutenant	9/17/1977	9/13/2002
				Lauer, J.	Volunteer		
				Lauer, Robert E.	Fire Fighter	3/9/1991	4/5/1991

Members of the West Allis Fire Department Past and Present

Name	Rank	Start	End
Lauer, J.	Volunteer	3/9/1991	- 4/5/1991
Lauer, Robert E.	Fire Fighter	5/11/1998	- 6/13/1998
Lazarski, Daniel R.	Fire Fighter	9/17/1977	- Present
Lazewski, Peter J.	Fire Fighter	4/8/1995	- Present
Ledvorowski, Daniel S.	Volunteer		
Leibenthal, C.	Fire Fighter	1/1/1925	- 10/10/1925
Leideritz, Harry G.	Volunteer		
Leitske, Henry	Lieutenant	1/19/1985	- Present
Lenske, Gregory D.	Fire Fighter	1/14/1984	- Present
Levenhagen, Chris P.	Lieutenant	3/2/1985	- Present
Levenhagen, Daniel E.	Equipment Operator	1/9/1988	- Present
Levenhagen, Joseph M.	Equipment Operator	3/29/1980	- Present
Levenhagen, Thomas P.	Captain	6/13/1959	- 5/6/1988
Liedle, Donald C.	Fire Fighter	4/26/1954	- 8/1/1970
Liefer, Bruce	Captain	10/23/1946	- 4/30/1984
Liska, Edward J.	Fire Fighter	10/7/2002	- Present
Liska, Scott	Volunteer		
Loebel, A.	Captain	6/15/1940	- 6/27/1961
Loiacano, Peter	Lieutenant	3/16/1950	- 5/25/1981
Lopac, Clarence M.	Assistant Chief	2/1/1924	- 1/10/1958
Luckow, Florian	Volunteer		
Luckow, W.	Captain	6/13/1959	- 1/4/1988
Luecht, Robert E.	Fire Fighter	4/4/1964	- 12/4/1966
Lund, Niles, M.	Alarm Operator	8/13/1955	- 5/31/1974
Luther, James R.	Equipment Operator	8/16/1954	- 2/17/1986
Lyles, Daniel F.	Lieutenant	4/18/1987	- Present
Machowski, Daniel R.	Fire Fighter	2/28/1998	- Present
Madden, Michael D.	Fire Fighter	6/25/2001	- Present
Maly, Curt	Volunteer	4/26/1954	- 7/16/1973
Mantey, Robert	Fire Fighter		
Marks, N.			
Marquis, Mark	Fire Fighter	10/7/2002	- 11/1/2002
Marz, August	Assistant Chief	11/25/1927	- 8/28/1965
Matter, Gerald C.	Deputy Chief	4/15/1967	- 4/20/1998
Matz, Herman	Lieutenant	2/12/1908	- 10/1/1932
May, W.	Volunteer		
McCarthy, Emmet J.	Fire Fighter	7/24/1993	- Present
McCorkle M.D., S. C.	Dept. Surgeon	5/15/1906	
McFadden, James R. Jr.	Fire Fighter	3/2/1985	- 11/27/1985
McGuire, Matthew R.	Fire Fighter	6/25/2001	- 5/25/2002
McMicken, A.	Volunteer		
Meade, Edward A.	Fire Fighter	2/28/1998	- 6/23/2003
Meier, Joel A.	Equipment Operator	1/25/1992	- Present
Meigs, H.	Volunteer		
Mellor, Charles P.	Deputy Chief	8/23/1954	- 1/4/1988
Menne, Harry H. Jr.	Fire Fighter	12/20/1958	- 12/28/1986
Merchant, Abel	Fire Fighter	5/15/1926	- 7/2/1951
Merville, John	Volunteer		
Meyer, A. R.	Volunteer		
Meyer, August	Volunteer		
Meyer, R. Sr.	Volunteer		
Mezydlo, Ralph	Captain	10/16/1946	- 3/28/1980
Miller, Craig R.	Fire Fighter	2/10/1979	- 6/13/1980
Miller, D.	Volunteer		
Miller, Robert H.	Fire Fighter	1/1/1925	- 9/1/1935
Miller, Robert S. Sr.	Assistant Chief	5/15/1906	
Minturn, Donald S.	Captain	4/26/1954	- 8/13/1981
Morch, John B.	Chief	10/16/1946	- 7/27/1975
Morrow, Robert L.	Equipment Operator	2/16/1980	- 10/17/2005
Morser, F.	Volunteer		
Mortl, Edward	Fire Fighter	10/22/1951	- 11/5/1951
Mueller, Kenneth A.	Fire Fighter	8/13/1955	- 2/20/1964

Members of the West Allis Fire Department Past and Present

Name	Rank	Start		End
Mueller, Richard A.	Battalion Chief	3/27/1982	-	Present
Muenchow, Tom A.	Lieutenant	4/12/1984	-	Present
Neeb, E. J.	Captain	5/15/1906	-	
Neeb, F.	Volunteer			
Nelesen, Margaret	Clerk-Steno II	5/9/1959	-	6/15/1963
Nelson, Henry C.	Chief	6/16/1923	-	6/16/1963
Newman, Chester	Captain	2/1/1928	-	5/1/1953
Nolte, Gerald	Chief	1/16/1949	-	7/25/1977
Oleson, Todd A.	Fire Fighter	6/4/1988	-	Present
Olson, Edry	Fire Fighter	9/10/1955	-	10/17/1964
Olson, Scott	Fire Fighter	1/21/1989	-	2/2/1989
Oppmann, Frank	Fire Fighter	2/1/1924	-	7/1/1947
O'Reilly, Bernard J.	Captain	1/16/1948	-	8/4/1984
Ottow, Albert C.	Equipment Operator	1/6/1968	-	6/18/1999
Ottow, Darrol O.	Equipment Operator	4/26/1954	-	3/21/1981
Ottow, Wallace A.	Equipment Operator	8/13/1955	-	1/17/1989
Ottoway, Walter	Lieutenant	5/15/1906	-	
Owsianny, Ronald L.	Deputy Chief	4/15/1967	-	2/17/1997
Paider, Guy J.	Fire Fighter	3/30/1996	-	Present
Palasz, Nicholas J.	Fire Fighter	8/3/1998	-	Present
Parker, C.	Volunteer			
Paust, J.	Volunteer			
Pedersen, Joseph W.	Equipment Operator	1/16/1954	-	5/29/1984
Peters, J.	Volunteer			
Peterson, Barney	Fire Fighter	3/8/1915	-	5/10/1923
Peterson, Harold	Fire Fighter	5/24/1934	-	6/1/1945
Peterson, Steve	Fire Fighter	10/7/2002	-	Present
Petrich, John	Fire Fighter	3/5/1931	-	7/1/1955
Petrich, John A.	Equipment Operator	5/9/1959	-	3/18/1987
Petrie, John	Fire Fighter	2/21/1907	-	7/1/1945
Phalen, E.	Volunteer			
Phillips, J.	Volunteer			
Piechura, Robert F.	Assistant Chief	9/6/1980	-	Present
Pirlot, Keith J.	Lieutenant	5/14/1983	-	Present
Pishion, Carl	Assistant Chief	2/1/1928	-	10/31/1953
Pishion, Wilfred	Fire Fighter	5/15/1926	-	11/17/1927
Pitman, Craig	Fire Fighter	10/7/2002	-	Present
Pogorzelski, Jerome M.	Fire Fighter	4/20/1963	-	6/17/1990
Pohlman, William	Fire Fighter	2/1/1930	-	5/1/1952
Ponzi, James J.	Equipment Operator	3/2/1985	-	Present
Poole, Walter	Fire Fighter	5/1/1927	-	5/16/1949
Pooler, Mason	Fire Fighter	10/7/2002	-	Present
Portz, Scott W.	Fire Fighter	8/3/1998	-	Present
Potkay, Brian M.	Captain	1/19/1985	-	Present
Potochich, Bruce E.	Fire Fighter	9/5/2000	-	Present
Potochich, Robert R.	Equipment Operator	2/6/1960	-	3/17/1989
Potzner, Audie F.	Fire Fighter	4/26/1954	-	6/8/1968
Radtke, C.	Volunteer			
Redmond, Gerald F.	Battalion Chief	3/16/1953	-	1/17/1985
Reikowski, Conrad R.	Equipment Operator	3/16/1953	-	3/18/1983
Reinke, Christoph C.	Captain	6/12/1982	-	Present
Rice, George H.	Lieutenant	9/16/1954	-	1/17/1987
Rock, M.	Volunteer			
Roedel, Richard P.	Battalion Chief	8/16/1954	-	1/3/1988
Rohde, Peter D.	Captain	3/19/1983	-	Present
Rohn, W.	Volunteer			
Rosenberg, Ronald R.	Equipment Operator	9/18/1965	-	1/19/1992
Roszak, John	Fire Fighter	4/15/1930	-	5/22/1952
Rounds, E.	Volunteer			
Ruidl, Otto J.	Fire Fighter	2/1/1924	-	10/1/1924
Rutley, Michael	Fire Fighter	1/25/1992	-	3/25/1993
Sabow, Robert L.	Fire Fighter	4/26/1954	-	5/29/1967
Sbonik, John R.	Captain	5/24/1975	-	1/6/2005

Members of the West Allis Fire Department Past and Present

Name	Rank	Start	End		Name	Rank	Start	End
Scharfenberg, Japeth D.	Fire Fighter	5/3/1999	-	Present	Socha, Joseph	Lieutenant	1/16/1949	-	1/18/1982
Schauz, Michael J.	Captain	2/19/1983	-	Present	Solowicz, Clement James	Equipment Operator	7/7/1951	-	4/13/1963
Scherer, P.	Volunteer				Sommers, M.	Volunteer		
Schieffelbein, James D.	Fire Fighter	10/1/1966	-	11/24/1977	Sparacino, Antonio J.	Captain	5/16/1949	-	6/19/1983
Schilz, Richard S.	Equipment Operator	4/7/1984	-	Present	Sparacino, Peter	Fire Fighter	1/16/1954	-	9/3/1980
Schimming, Patrick	Fire Fighter	2/13/1942	-	7/15/1975	Sperka, Thomas	Lieutenant	6/13/1959	-	1/30/1986
Schmitt, James A.	Equipment Operator	7/27/1963	-	10/12/1991	Stanwood, Bruce G.	Lieutenant	6/22/1985	-	Present
Schoen, Elmer	Fire Fighter	2/1/1924	-	7/15/1946	Staszak, Chad J.	Fire Fighter	5/3/1999	-	Present
Schoenborn, Robert T.	Deputy Chief	11/6/1971	-	7/1/2002	Stauffer, David	Fire Fighter	4/15/1967	-	4/25/1968
Scholtz, Herbert	Lieutenant	1/1/1944	-	2/28/1975	Steffen, Walter	Fire Fighter	11/23/1925	-	7/2/1941
Schrader, Raymond E.	Chief	4/15/1967	-	4/20/1998	Stenz, Richard J. Jr.	Lieutenant	6/2/1984	-	Present
Schrieber, Brent W.	Fire Fighter	2/28/1998	-	Present	Sterzinger, J.	Volunteer		
Schubert, John	Equipment Operator	11/9/1953	-	1/13/1980	Stiglitz, Mallory E.	Fire Fighter	8/1/2005	-	Present
Schuenke, Gerald	Fire Fighter	10/12/1957	-	4/3/1984	Strassman, Roger J.	Captain	1/9/1965	-	1/24/1992
Schulte, J.	Volunteer				Streicher, Gary A.	Assistant Chief	3/19/1983	-	Present
Schultz, Charles	Fire Fighter	10/1/1924	-	12/17/1947	Streit, Charles R.	Fire Fighter	5/10/1958	-	5/9/1959
Schulze, H.	Volunteer				Strickler, Donald A.	Captain	7/12/1980	-	Present
Schumacher, Robert W.	Equipment Operator	1/13/1968	-	1/31/1998	Strom, Floyd	Captain	1/16/1949	-	1/17/1981
Schunk, G.	Volunteer				Stuart, Byron	Volunteer		
Schwartz, Douglas W.	Equipment Operator	7/7/1951	-	1/17/1981	Stuart, H.	Volunteer		
Schwiner, John T.	Fire Fighter	11/3/1984	-	6/18/2004	Sura, Mark	Fire Fighter	10/7/2002	-	Present
Seegar, William	Volunteer				Sweek, Terry L.	Lieutenant	6/13/1959	-	6/26/1989
Seltrecht, Truman C.	Fire Fighter	9/10/1955	-	1/18/1987	Tenant, Keith J.	Fire Fighter	12/17/1966	-	3/17/1997
Shakula, David A.	Equipment Operator	4/2/1966	-	3/3/1995	Teresinski, Donald E.	Equipment Operator	2/6/1960	-	2/12/1985
Shakula, Robert H.	Captain	6/29/1959	-	1/20/1991	Tess, Robert E.	Battalion Chief	3/6/1952	-	1/18/1983
Shinkle, Thomas M.	Lieutenant	7/29/1989	-	Present	Tewes, Ben	Fire Fighter	2/1/1930	-	11/15/1952
Simonet, F.	Volunteer				Tewes, Eugene E.	Fire Fighter	9/10/1955	-	4/18/1959
Siuda, Arthur	Lieutenant	6/15/1940	-	9/26/1971	Theim, Michael J.	Fire Fighter	5/3/1999	-	Present
Smrz, Jerold	Fire Fighter	6/13/1959	-	5/27/1967	Tickler, R.	Volunteer		
Snow, David J.	Fire Fighter	2/14/1987	-	Present	Toepfer, Eric J.	Equipment Operator	3/5/1988	-	Present
Snow, Jeffrey, J.	Fire Fighter	8/13/1983	-	Present	Tomczak, Mark J.	Captain	3/2/1985	-	Present

Members of the West Allis Fire Department
Past and Present

Name	Position	From	To
Trokan, Paul	Equipment Operator	9/13/1958	7/23/1983
Unz, Timothy R.	Lieutenant	8/3/1974	12/29/2001
Valona, Donald J.	Battalion Chief	12/17/1966	7/18/1998
Van Huecklin, B.	Volunteer		
Verhalen, Duane A.	Fire Fighter	10/29/1977	12/3/1991
Vicena, Marlene	Secretary	5/9/1959	6/14/1963
Vieau, Ralph A. Jr.	Civ. Alarm Operator	9/10/1973	
Vieau, Ralph A. Sr.	Fire Inspector	9/10/1955	6/1/1988
Viel, Wayne D.	Equipment Operator	4/26/1954	5/17/1985
Vogel, Melvin J.	Fire Fighter	2/1/1930	2/8/1930
Volk, Dion D.	Equipment Operator	9/12/1987	Present
Vopal, Irene E.	Clerk-Stenographer	4/28/1954	4/10/1959
Vorpagel, Timothy W.	Lieutenant	11/30/1991	Present
Walloch, Donald J.	Captain	8/30/1975	3/2/2002
Wasweiler, W.	Volunteer		
Weber, J.	Volunteer		
Weber, Ruth	Clerk-Stenographer	4/1/1952	5/9/1952
Wendt, Mark R.	Equipment Operator	7/29/1989	Present
Wenzel, Michael J.	Fire Fighter	4/16/1954	6/17/1959
Werner, Russel A.	Fire Fighter	1/19/1980	Present
Westover, Harlan R.	Battalion Chief	1/4/1969	12/25/1999
Wichser, Ralph	Equipment Operator	3/6/1952	3/15/1965
Wickersheimer, Guy M.	Fire Fighter	5/18/1985	Present
Wiedel, Jeffrey J.	Lieutenant	4/18/1987	Present
Wininger, Leo D.	Fire Fighter	2/6/1960	1/5/1978
Winter, John R.	Equipment Operator	8/13/1955	4/13/1968
Witcher, I.	Volunteer		
Witt, Barry R.	Lieutenant	11/17/1979	8/29/2003
Witt, Charlene	Principal Secretary	1/4/1982	Present
Wright, S.	Volunteer		
Yonker, Melvin H.	Equipment Operator	4/26/1954	11/11/1966
Zajdel, James M.	Lieutenant	3/2/1985	Present
Zalar, Frank A.	Battalion Chief	7/22/1967	10/31/1998
Zellmann, Kurt W.	Fire Fighter	8/2/2004	Present
Zepezauer, Edward M.	Captain	4/26/1954	3/10/1983
Ziolecki, Chris R.	Fire Fighter	3/24/1989	Present
Zyniel, Edward P.	Lieutenant	3/5/1931	10/11/1952

Coops and Interns

Name	Position	From	To
Berg, Kaylinn	Clerk/Intern	2002	2003
Cady, Amanda	Clerk/Intern	1996	2001
Fischer, Greg	Clerk/Intern	2001	2002
Kaltenberg, Steven J.	MATC Fire Intern	2005	
Schalk, Angela	Clerk/Intern	2003	2004
Winiarski, Grace	Clerk/Intern	2004	2005
Zimpel, Alana	Clerk/Intern	2005	Present

Members of the West Allis Board of Police and Fire Commissioners

Commissioner	From	to	Commissioner	From	to
Velser, C. W.			Church, Howard	1948	1971
Levy, Henry			Dombrovske, Norbert	1960	1972
Meigs, Henry			Glojek, F.	1963	1973
Fisher, William A.			Mundingler, A.	1964	1974
Ehrke, Gustave		1937	Canavan, Dr. James H.	1970	1980
Mueller, Theodore		1938	Calhoun, B.	1971	1976
Glojek, Ferdinand		1938	Krafcheck, A.	1972	1977
Huntington, Steve		1939	Panozuan, Charles	1973	1978
Phalen, Eugene		1940	Snow, James	1974	1984
Karasiewisz, Anthony	1937	1960	Kastner, Art	1976	1981
Hohler, Walter	1938	1941	Schuch, Norm	1977	1982
Schnaufer, John	1938	1963	Beitzinger, Larry	1978	1988
Froelich, William	1939	1944	Huber, Robert T.	1980	1990
Rausch, Francis	1940	1970	Hislop Jr., Reginald T.	1981	1986
Zilles, Norbert	1941	1946	Ostrenga, Raymond I.	1982	1992
Bartman, Clyde	1946	1948	Lelinski, Charles J.	1984	1989
Mundingler, Richard	1944	1964	Mike, Michael J.	1986	1996

Members of the West Allis Board of Police and Fire Commissioners

Commissioner	From		to
Snow, James	1988	-	1993
Fuhr, Harlow	1989	-	1994
Canavan, James	1990	-	1995
Facchinello, Lee	1992	-	2001
Wendtland, Vernon	1993	-	1998
Clark, Wayne B.	1994	-	2004
Kramer, Rev. Gerald	1995	-	2002
Baldwin, Leverett	1996	-	1996
Maren, Kenneth	1996	-	2001
Zidar, Robert	1998	-	2001
Dagenhardt, Kathleen	2001	-	Present
Nelson, Janet	2001	-	Present
Keever, Edward F.	2001	-	Present
Kempen, Joseph	2002	-	Present
Haass, Kevin	2004	-	Present

WA Police and Fire Commissioners, 1944

WA Board of Police and Fire Commissioners, 2006
Edward F. Keever, Janet Nelson, Joseph Kempen, Kathleen Dagenhardt, Kevin Haass

Chapter 7

Scrapbook

Dummy rescue

Things aren't exactly as they appear when West Allis firefighter Robert Kurziak carries the figure of a woman from a burning building at 8020 W. National Ave. Kurziak pulled a mannequin from the structure, which housed a photo studio, a dress shop and several apartments. The three-alarm fire Monday destroyed the building. At least one person suffered minor injuries. / Story on 6A

MICHAEL SEARS / Sentinel photographer

In a scene from the movie "Backdraft", a rookie Chicago firefighter rescued a mannequin from a burning building and was teased by other firefighters. Shortly afterward, West Allis Firefighter Bob Kurziak was photographed with a mannequin from a retail store fire on W. National Avenue. Milwaukee Sentinel photographer Michael Sears captured the moment.

THE MILWAUKEE JOURNAL

Local News, Picture Page, Sports — Tuesday, March 22, 1955 — TV and R:

As can be seen in these pictures, Sparky is no ordinary dog. She is the mascot at the West Allis No. 2 fire station, 1460 S. 108th st. Firemen there have taught her a variety of tricks. Among them are sitting at a desk, drinking from a water fountain and opening doors. The 10 month old dog likes to sit in the fire truck, but she doesn't ride to fires. She is shown with Merlin Kolberg, 800 S. 58th st., West Allis.

4/16/2005 Franklin Dump Fire

P. Richard Eells Photo

9/19/2003

193

New fire fighters

Acting Fire Chief Robert Block (left) stands next to probationary fire fighters David Lau and Peter Lazewski with Dr. James Canavan, vice president of the West Allis Police and Fire Commission. Lau and Lazewski were hired by the department recently to fill vacancies caused by retirement and resignation.

201

www.ingramcontent.com/pod-product-compliance
Lightning Source LLC
Chambersburg PA
CBHW081916180426
43198CB00038B/2871